# GREAT Tween Getaways

# Getaways

# 8 Retreats for Tweens

**Marcey Balcomb**

Abingdon's
**Great Tween Getaways**
**8 Retreats for Tweens**

ISBN 0-687-49470-2

06 07 08 09 10 11 12 13 14 15—10 9 8 7 6 5 4 3 2 1

MANUFACTURED IN THE UNITED STATES OF AMERICA

# Contents

## About the Writer:

**Marcey Balcomb**

is a 32-year veteran in youth ministry in The United Methodist Church. She is currently Director of Common Cup Youth Ministry, a cooperative program in Portland, Oregon, and youth specialist with the OR-ID Conference Youth Ministry Team.

Marcey is co-author of *Twists of Faith: Ministry with Youth at the Turning Points of their Lives*; author of *Flip the Switch* (*Faith in Motion* series); author of *Single Digit Youth Groups: Working with Fewer than Ten Teens*; co-author of *Combos 3*; and author of *Single Digit Youth Groups 2* . She has also written for *YouthNet, LinC, Connect, Devo'Zine, WITH, Interpreter, Circuit Rider*, and others.

### Gene Roehlkepartain

is Senior Advisor, Office of the President for the Search Institute in Minneapolis, Minnesota.

# Messy Moments

Life is exhilarating and scary for children in the upper elementary grades. On the one hand, they're gaining confidence, expanding their horizons, doing more things on their own. On the other hand, they're experiencing the pain of bullies, the disappointment of failure, and the fear of entering unknown places. Those of us watching from the safety of adulthood see our little children begin to show signs of adolescence. During this time of life, write my research colleagues at Search Institute, "children have one foot firmly planted in childhood, and the other gingerly reaching toward the vastly different world of adolescence."

How do we help children navigate this transition? It can be easy to spend time worrying and wishing that the natural process of growth and development would somehow shift just this once. But Search Institute's framework of Developmental Assets offers a different, more proactive approach. It identifies forty positive building blocks of development that researchers have found increase the odds that young people will grow up successfully and avoid many of the risky behaviors that become all too common in adolescence.

*Great Tween Getaways: Eight Retreats for Tweens* introduces you to some of these developmental assets and gives the creative ideas and practical steps you'll need to address specific asset-building themes through relevant, creative retreats grounded in Christian traditions and practices. It is important to remember, though, that the explicit content of what you "teach" during the retreat is only a small part of what children learn and experience. Yes, you want them to learn about family support, positive peer influence, and resistance skills (three of the forty assets). But it's probably even more important that they experience love and support from caring adults in their church family; that they discover what it's like to influence their peers positively; and that they experience working through challenges or conflicts together with love, patience, creativity, and a good dose of humor.

In other words, not only can your retreats be about assets, but they can also be opportunities for young people to experience the assets. Retreats can offer a safe, trusting place away from the routines and habits that sometimes distract from positive change and growth. That kind of asset building happens when you are more attentive to the children than to the notebook. It happens when you focus more attention on getting to know something new about each child than on trying to get them to learn a new song or how to stand when they shoot a free throw. It happens when you're as interested in listening to them as you are in insisting they listen to you.

Sometimes people look at the framework of Developmental Assets (which is provided on page 95) and think it's all so neat and orderly and tidy—something else we can organize, strategize, and check off the list. But real life is much messier than that. Real life means that some children will struggle with communicating with parents (asset #2), while others will be so busy that they never spend time at home (asset #20). Some will feel safe at home and in their neighborhood (asset #10), but others will rarely experience conflicts being resolved peacefully (asset #36). So we can't just learn them, check them off, and be done with it. Indeed, sometimes children are so caught up in the messiness of real life, they can't even notice the assets that are present all around them and within them.

That's where retreats come in. For a day or two, children are away from the noise, the conflicting signals, and the pressures. If you're thoughtful and intentional about it, they spend enough time to slow down and open up. In those moments they see one another and themselves in new, deeper ways. They gain new perspective on the gifts in their families, church, schools, neighborhoods, and communities. They can discover more about who they are, what they value, and who they are becoming. In those moments they can recognize that they have something valuable to share with one another and the world.

Like the life experiences of these changing children-becoming-teenagers, these times are messy. They're unpredictable. They're scary. They're joyful.

These are asset-building moments. These are holy moments.

Eugene C. Roehlkepartain
Search Institute, Minneapolis, Minnesota

# Introduction: Value of Retreats

**RETREATS** are an extended length of time, often in a natural setting apart from our regular settings, where an individual or a particular grouping goes to reflect, to renew, and to grow. In the Christian tradition it is also a time and a place for meditation and prayer, for learning, for joining in Christian conversation, and for having experiences that help us deepen our faith and grow closer to God. The experience of being on retreat is often a time when people make decisions about changes in their lives, or make commitments to expand their spiritual practices when they return to daily life. By helping kids develop assets in a retreat setting, we also show them the value of being on retreat to focus on whatever they are dealing with or wanting to learn in their lives. And sometimes in the midst of a place apart, they discover God tugging them to find deeper meaning in their lives through communion with nature and with other people of faith.

## The Value of Assets Building

Developmental Assets are positive factors in young people, families, communities, schools, and other settings that have been found to be important in promoting young people's healthy development. So what is it that we should be supplying our young people with in order that they might be responsible, effective, and caring members of society? The activities in this book will help you understand some of the core elements of asset building, and will lead the young people through some common experiences that help them grow. Some assets are internal—instinctive or learned ways of choosing appropriate behavior, making wise decisions, solving problems, and much more. Other assets are external and rely on other people providing opportunities for new experiences and stable life settings. The support of family, church, community, and peers and good communications are critical elements in helping tweens become strong, self-sufficient, confident, and caring people.

## Biblical and Theological/Spiritual Basis for Asset Retreats

It is our responsibility, and our honor, to care for the children in our homes, churches, and communities. Their key learning is from observing and experiencing their own family life, and they tend to emulate what they have seen and experienced. It is easy to derive, then, that their thinking and behavior will be similar to that which they learned while growing up. Therefore, we must live in the way of right and good. The Book of Proverbs tells us as much in several Scriptures.

- Proverbs 22:6 says: "Train children in the right way, and when old, they will not stray."
- Proverbs 20:7 says: "The righteous walk in integrity—happy are the children who follow them!"
- Proverbs 20:11 says: "Even children make themselves known by their acts, by whether what they do is pure and right."

If we ever have difficulty choosing to live in the light of Christ, we need only to think of the children for whom we set an example by our decisions and behavior. They observe us any time we are present, not just when we are in a class or group activity. There is no down time or separate lifestyle when living the life of a disciple of Jesus Christ. Our faith and our life are one. It is up to us to teach our children how to live well.

# Organizing Retreats

**Each retreat includes:**
- schedule
- preparation
- list of supplies
- list of food needed
- Scripture and reflection
- icebreaker
- retreat activities, including Bible study
- closing celebration
- reproducible pages for some activities

## Tips for Recruiting
There are several ways to go about recruiting both leaders and participants for retreats and other events. Here are a few suggestions to consider in your process:

*Recruiting Adults:*
- Ask some of the tweens who attend regularly for names of adults they enjoy being around and think would be good chaperones and leaders for their group. Have them nominate these people.
- Prepare a list of nominated persons, starting the list with the ones who seem most suitable for your available positions. (Even if the tweens nominate someone, you need to evaluate whether or not you feel this person would be good in the position for which you are trying to recruit.)
- Prepare a written list of information you will want to share with the people you contact.
- Contact people to tell them that the tweens have nominated them to be adult workers for a retreat or a series of retreats.
- Be ready to tell the adults what will be expected of them.
- Give them a time period to make a decision, rather than making them answer on the spot. If they indicate that they are unavailable but are interested in the retreats, ask if you can contact them for a future event. If they say yes, put them on a list of potential adults for the future.

Once a person is recruited, he or she should be given a Volunteer Disclosure Form or other document for your use in determining whether or not it is appropriate for that person to be working with young people. (This varies from state to state and church to church; check with your church office.) This, of course, means you must plan ahead when recruiting. The only last-minute recruits should be those filling in for others who must cancel. You may be able to avoid this by recruiting an extra male and extra female to be on standby or on call.

*Recruiting Tweens:*
- Have the basic retreat information in front of you when contacting the tweens.
- Be ready to tell them a couple of highlights they can expect during the retreat.
- Ask their parents to talk with them about this special event and to encourage their child(ren) to attend.
- Be ready to explain financial obligations and what assistance is available, if needed.

## Promotion/Advertising

Getting the attention of people, especially busy and active people, takes multiple contacts in a variety of ways. When it comes to retreats, it not only involves the young people and their schedules but also affects their families and those schedules. Planning ahead is crucial in order to allow enough time both to get young people's attention and to get them to respond. You still have all the other work to complete the process. So start early!

## Here are some steps that may help you:

Determine a few basic key elements people will want to know when they first hear about the retreat. Think of what questions you would ask if you were the parent of a tween.

1. The first notification should be verbal. Make an announcement to the tweens and their parents in person when at all possible, so they are not surprised by the information and they know to watch for more details.

2. The second notification may be by e-mail or postal service and should include:
   - Title of the retreat.
   - Date, day, and time.
   - Who is it for? What grades, ages, genders, are invited?
   - Location of the event.
   - Cost.
   - How and when to register (registration form may or may not be with this first notification).

3. The third notification may be by e-mail and postal service and should include:
   - Title of the retreat.
   - Date, day, and time.
   - Who is it for? What grades, ages, genders, are invited?
   - Location of event.
   - Cost.
   - Time group will gather to load the vehicle(s); time you will leave for your destination; time you will return.
   - Address and emergency contact phone number and name.
   - Purpose of the retreat.
   - Scheduled highlights (as opposed to a detailed schedule).
   - Names of the responsible adults attending.
   - Description of the transportation arrangements.
   - List of what to bring.
   - How and when to register.

## Other Important Information

It will be important to have a conversation and some discussion to help the tweens understand the importance of each person agreeing to behavioral standards that benefit the group, both now and on the retreat.

You will need everyone to have signed parental permission to attend the retreat. You may use the permission form on page 96 or one of your own. One form can include permission for a full year.

# ONE-DAY RETREATS

The retreat schedules are a guideline of how to fit various items into the day. The length of any activity can vary greatly from group to group. You are encouraged to adjust the schedule to fit your group's needs.

It will also be important to allow some free time between some activities, especially with this age level. Their attention span is limited, so many activities will tend to go more quickly than expected.

Have additional appropriate things for tweens to do during free time. This can be a good group-building time, simply by having them spend extended time together.

It is also important to have some rest time, even in a one-day retreat. Don't forget to provide lots of water. Developing bodies and brains need it!

# **1** Resisting Temptation

---

## SCHEDULE

| | | | | |
|---|---|---|---|---|
| 9:00 a.m. | Registration | | 12:45 p.m. | Break |
| 9:20 a.m. | Icebreaker | | 1:05 p.m. | Rest |
| 9:35 a.m. | Introduction to retreat topic | | 1:25 p.m. | Activity 5 |
| 9:40 a.m. | Activity 1 | | 2:00 p.m. | Activity 6 |
| 10:00 a.m. | Juice break | | 2:30 p.m. | Snack |
| 10:05 a.m. | Activity 2 | | 2:45 p.m. | Activity 7 |
| 10:30 a.m. | Activity 3 | | 3:30 p.m. | Clean up/Pack up |
| 10:45 a.m. | Free time | | 3:50 p.m. | Activity 8 |
| 11:00 a.m. | Activity 4 | | 4:15 p.m. | Closing celebration |
| 11:30 a.m. | Lunch preparation (part of the program) | | 4:30 p.m. | Parents pick up tweens |
| 12:00 noon | Lunch | | | |

---

## Supplies

- NRSV Bibles
- retreat instructions and printed materials
- nametags or materials to make them
- easel pad or other large sheets of paper
- markers
- masking tape
- paper for each person
- pen for each person
- food service items: plates, cups, napkins, spoons

*(Note: Specific items for each activity are listed by activity.)*

## Food

**Mid-morning break:**
- juice

**Lunch:**
- sandwich
- carrot sticks
- fruit
- chips
- cookie
- drink

**Afternoon snack suggestions:**
- yogurt
- crackers
- cheese
- juice
- bottled water

# 1 Resisting Temptation

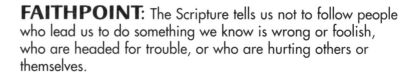

**FAITHPOINT:** The Scripture tells us not to follow people who lead us to do something we know is wrong or foolish, who are headed for trouble, or who are hurting others or themselves.

**SCRIPTURE:** Psalm 119:64-68 and Deuteronomy 5:7-22.

## SCRIPTURE REFLECTION:
It will be important, when working with this retreat topic, for tweens to realize the difference between hanging out with people who are a bad influence, and caring about those people because they are children of God. There is much to be learned and gained from spending time with persons who are different from us; but when it leads to behaving badly or making unwise choices, it is better not to be overly influenced by them. The easiest way to discourage their poor influence is to avoid hanging around with them. Greeting someone politely at school is appropriate, but extended time with them may be detrimental.

Instead of following people who would lead them astray, tweens can learn to encourage others to take a better path (the path God would have us follow) and give them good advice.

The Bible gives us direction as to what path we are to take.

## PREPARATION:
See page 11 for the preparation check list.

## ICEBREAKER: PEOPLE BINGO
The goal of this game is for each tween to get a different signature in each square on **Reproducible 1A**. (If the number of participants in the retreat is fewer than the number of squares, just have them get as many as possible.) We have left you a few free blanks so that you can add some that will more closely mirror your tweens. Fill these spaces in before printing.

## ACTIVITY 1: FOLLOW THE LEADER
Play the traditional children's game of Follow the Leader.

Ask for a volunteer to be the first leader. The group should line up behind the leader, leaving enough room behind each person for whatever "travel activity" the leader chooses.

## People Bingo
**Supplies:**
- Reproducible 1A, page 17
- pens or pencils

**Preparation:**
- Gather supplies.
- Photocopy Reproducible 1A for each person.

## Follow the Leader
**Supplies:**
- Reproducible 1B, page 18

**Preparation:**
- Photocopy Reproducible 1B for every three tweens.

After one minute, have the leader go to the back of the line, and let the next person in line lead.

After one minute, switch leaders again. If your group is large, you may need to have multiple games going simultaneously, instead of one group.

After playing for about ten minutes, call the group back together and ask them to sit in groups of three.

Ask the group if they have any comments about what they just did, and give them a chance to respond.

Hand out the examples sheet on **Reproducible 1B**, one per group of three, and tell them to discuss briefly each example within their group. (Give them up to ten minutes for these discussions, but end sooner if they are finished.)

## ACTIVITY 2: BIBLE STUDY

Have the tweens take turns reading the Scriptures on **Reproducible 1C**. Invite them to come up with one sentence that describes, in their own language, what each Scripture means to them. Each Scripture includes conversation helps, if needed.

You may meet in smaller groups for these discussions.

**Say: Every day you make choices about what you will or won't do. It is difficult to always choose the right thing to do. When you have an opportunity to choose to do something wrong or dangerous, remember that you are strong enough to resist. Following the leader may often be the right thing to do, but if the leader does things that are wrong, you can choose *not* to hang around with that person. It is your own responsibility to make a good choice.**

## ACTIVITY 3: CARVED IN STONE

Read aloud Deuteronomy 5:7-14a, 16-22 as printed on the following page (from *The Message*).

## Bible Study
Supplies:
• Reproducible 1C, page 19
• pens or pencils

Preparation:
Photocopy Reproducible 1C for each person.

## Carved in Stone
Supplies:
• Reproducible 1D, page 20
• pens or pencils

Preparation:
• Gather supplies.
• Photocopy Reproducible 1D for each person.

## Simon Says Rules
- Players form a line (or lines) across the play space facing the leader.
- The leader says "Simon says, (*whatever the action is*)" and begins doing the action. The players imitate what Simon does until the next instruction is given.
- Then the leader quickly says "Simon says," gives a new instruction, and begins a new action; players imitate the action.
- At some point the leader says and does an action without first saying "Simon says," and whoever imitates it is out of the game.
- The game continues until one player is left.

### Game
**Supplies:**
- Bible

**Preparation:**
- none

No other gods, only me.

No carved gods of any size, shape, or form of anything whatever, whether of things that fly or walk or swim. Don't bow down to them and don't serve them because I am God, your God, and I'm a most jealous God. I hold parents responsible for any sins they pass onto their children to the third, and yes, even to the fourth generation. But I'm lovingly loyal to the thousands who love me and keep my commandments.

No using the name of God, your God, in curses or silly banter; God won't put up with the irreverent use of his name.

No working on the Sabbath; keep it holy just as God, your God, commanded you. Work six days, doing everything you have to do, but the seventh day is a Sabbath, a Rest Day—no work.

Respect your father and mother—God, your God, commands it! You'll have a long life; the land that God is giving you will treat you well.

No murder.

No adultery.

No stealing.

No lies about your neighbor.

No coveting your neighbor's wife. And no lusting for his house, field, servant, maid, ox, or donkey either—nothing that belongs to your neighbor.

These are the words that God spoke to the whole congregation at the mountain. He spoke in a tremendous voice from the fire and cloud and dark mist. And that was it. No more words. Then he wrote them on two slabs of stone and gave them to me. (Deuteronomy 5:7-14a, 16-22, The Message)

Hand out **Reproducible 1D**. Read aloud the instructions at the top of the sheet and invite the tweens to begin.

## ACTIVITY 4: GAME (outdoors, if possible)
Read Proverbs 12:26.

Say: This Scripture is a reminder not to follow people who would lead you astray, but rather to give them good advice and to encourage them to take a better path.

Play "Simon Says." Describe the game in case someone doesn't know how to play or knows different rules to the game. Play for ten to fifteen minutes. Ask tweens to give you a few examples of something they would *not* be willing to do just because Simon said to do it.

**Leader's Tip**: Give them a restroom break before the next activity.

## ACTIVITY 5: INFLUENCES
Hand out a copy of the worksheet **Reproducible 1E** to each person.

After the students have completed these, invite a brief conversation about their answers.

## ACTIVITY 6: STANDING FIRM BIBLE STUDY
Divide participants into four groups.

Give each group one of the Scriptures from **Reproducible 1F**.

Each group should create one scenario, in today's language, describing a situation with tweens that portrays the Scripture message. Then they are to make it into a short skit to present to the other groups.

Allow about five minutes for their skit development.

Then ask each group to perform their skit for the rest of the groups.

## ACTIVITY 7: SMALL GROUP
Divide tweens into groups of four or five. Shuffle the conversation cards (**Reproducible 1G**) for each group so the cards are in random order. Instruct each group to sit in a circle and place the stack of cards upside down in the middle. Invite each student in the groups to draw one card at a time and respond to the statement with "OK" or "Not OK." Have them talk briefly about any statements that get their attention.

### Influences
**Supplies:**
- Reproducible 1E, page 21
- pens or pencils

**Preparation:**
- Photocopy Reproducible 1E for each person.

### Standing Firm Bible Study
**Supplies:**
- Reproducible 1F page, 21
- scissors

**Preparation:**
- Photocopy Reproducible 1F and cut apart the Scriptures.

### Small Group
**Supplies:**
- Reproducible 1G, page 22
- scissors

**Preparation:**
- Photocopy Reproducible 1D and cut out the conversation cards, one set for each group of 4–5 kids.

## Standing Firm Covenant

**Supplies:**
- Bibles
- pens or pencils
- small pieces of paper

**Preparation:**
- Cut paper into small pieces (approximately half of a regular sheet of paper).

## Closing Celebration

**Supplies:**
- Bibles
- commandments created in Activity 3
- candle
- matches
- bowl or basket

**Preparation:**
- none

## ACTIVITY 8: STANDING FIRM COVENANT

Read aloud Psalm 119:64-68.

**Say:** This is a plea to God and a reminder for you to follow God rather than following people who lead you into problems and trouble.

Pass out a small piece of paper and a pen for each person.

Ask participants to write MY COVENANT at the top, and to write one sentence about choosing to follow what they believe is right and not following someone who encourages them to do something wrong. It might be in the form of a prayer, if they wish.

Ask tweens to keep these covenants and put them in a place at home where they will see them.

## CLOSING CELEBRATION

Light a candle.

Read Psalm 119:64 out loud together.

**Say:** Offer your own commandments (from Activity 3) **to God by putting them all in the bowl** (*or basket*) **in the center of the celebration space.**

**Pray:** God, we are sorry for the times we make the wrong choice, even when we know what's right. We ask you to help us resist following others who are a bad influence. And we want to learn to be better influences on those around us. Help us to know what will be good, and to always choose the good. Amen.

# Bingo

| | | | |
|---|---|---|---|
| IS WEARING GLASSES | isn't wearing socks today | | knows the Lord's Prayer |
| used to live in a different state | likes the color red | plays soccer | HAS BEEN OUT OF THE UNITED STATES |
| has a pet bird | | has lived on or visited a farm | likes licorice ice cream |
| | likes math | enjoys cooking or baking | goes to your school |
| has brown eyes | | likes to sing | has two siblings |

**Great Tween Getaways**

# Follow the Leader Questions

*Would you willingly follow a person who did these things?*

- Rode a bike without a helmet.

- Sneaked in and climbed a radio station tower.

- Lied to a friend.

- Stole a candy bar from the grocery store.

- Made fun of other kids who are different.

- Drove a car before he or she had a permit or license.

- Watched a movie his or her parents said not to watch.

- Jumped off a low bridge into the river to go swimming.

- Cheated on a test at school.

- Smoked a cigarette because someone encouraged him or her to do it.

- Received too much money back in change from a purchase and didn't give it back.

- Downloaded music off the Internet illegally.

- Made rude comments about his or her teachers.

- Borrowed some money from a friend but never paid it back.

- Made prank phone calls to someone he or she didn't like.

- Whacked someone over the head with several sheets of rolled-up paper.

# Read the Scriptures

Psalm 119:64-68
*The earth, O LORD, is full of your steadfast love;
teach me your statutes. You have dealt well with your
servant, O LORD, according to your word. Teach me
good judgment and knowledge, for I believe in your
commandments. Before I was humbled I went astray,
but now I keep your word. You are good and do
good; teach me your statutes.*

* What are some things kids say to get others to
  follow them?

* What would it take to follow God rather than
  people who lead you into problems and trouble?

Proverbs 12:26
*The righteous gives good advice to friends, but the
way of the wicked leads astray.*

* What does it mean to be led astray?

* Instead of following people who would lead you
  astray—encourage them to take a better path and
  give them good advice.

1 Timothy 4:12
*Let no one despise your youth, but set the believers
an example in speech and conduct, in love, in faith,
in purity.*

* What are some examples of how you could set a
  good example?

* Instead of being a follower, be an example of a
  leader for others to follow.

Proverbs 10:9-10
*Whoever walks in integrity walks securely, but
whoever follows perverse ways will be found out.
Whoever winks the eye causes trouble, but the one
who rebukes boldly makes peace.*

* How hard is it to be the peacemaker instead of
  just standing by?

* Instead of just standing by and watching someone
  cause trouble, say something to encourage that
  person to stop.

Proverbs 20:7
*The righteous walk in integrity—happy are the
children who follow them!*

* What is integrity?

* Is it important?

* This is a reminder to choose to follow people who
  do what is right—those who are trustworthy and
  have integrity.

Luke 9:23-25
*Then he said to them all, "If any want to become my
followers, let them deny themselves and take up their
cross daily and follow me. For those who want to
save their life will lose it, and those who lose their
life for my sake will save it. What does it profit them
if they gain the whole world, but lose or forfeit
themselves?"*

* What does it mean for you to follow Jesus?

# Carved in Stone

_____'s Commandments
(name)

If you were to give your friends ten commandments based on the things you think are most important, which of these would you choose? Put an X by the best 10 on this stone tablet—or you may even want to label them in order of importance, 1 through 10, with 1 being the most important.

___ Don't lie.

___ Share what you have with others who need it more than you.

___ Don't hurt or injure others.

___ Love everyone, even if you don't like them.

___ Go to school.

___ Worship only God.

___ Don't use offensive language.

___ Use money wisely.

___ Don't cheat.

___ Spend time with people who are a good influence.

___ Don't use drugs.

___ Respect your family.

___ Learn as much as you can.

___ Don't have sex before you are ready to take responsibility for both physical and emotional results.

___ Take good care or our environment.

___ Don't take things that aren't yours.

___ Be kind and helpful to others.

___ Don't waste time.

___ Make good decisions.

___ Encourage your friends.

# Influences

**How often do you feel you are a good influence on the other kids around you?**

____ Almost always
____ A lot of the time
____ Sometimes
____ Not very often
____ Almost never

**Are you ever concerned that...**

| | Often | Sometimes | Not |
|---|---|---|---|
| your friends don't treat you well? | ____ | ____ | ____ |
| your parents won't like your friends? | ____ | ____ | ____ |
| your peers won't accept you? | ____ | ____ | ____ |
| your friends think you aren't cool? | ____ | ____ | ____ |
| a friend is a bad influence on you? | ____ | ____ | ____ |
| you might make wrong choices? | ____ | ____ | ____ |
| you can't resist following the crowd? | ____ | ____ | ____ |
| you're afraid to stand up for what's right? | | | |

# Words of Wisdom

Proverbs 12:26  The righteous gives good advice to friends, but the way of the wicked leads astray.

Matthew 24:4a  Jesus answered them, "Beware that no one leads you astray."

Proverbs 13:20  Whoever walks with the wise becomes wise, but the companion of fools suffers harm.

Proverbs 14:16  The wise are cautious and turn away from evil, but the fool throws off restraint and is careless.

# Conversation Cards

✂

| | |
|---|---|
| Talking about someone behind that person's back. | BEING SEXUALLY ACTIVE AS LONG AS YOU DON'T GO "ALL THE WAY." |
| Copying someone else's answers on a test as long as you don't get caught. | Taking something that isn't yours as long as it isn't worth a lot of money. |
| Telling racial or gender jokes when you think they're funny. | Keeping the change from a purchase when the clerk gives you back too much money. |
| Lying to someone rather than upsetting that person with the truth. | Keeping a secret that might result in someone being seriously harmed. |
| **Apologizing to someone in order to get him or her to stop bothering you.** | Turning in school work as your own, even though you copied it off the Internet. |
| **Cutting in line to join a friend rather than waiting your turn.** | Being nice to someone to gain something you want, such as popularity or influence. |
| Drinking alcohol before you're legally old enough as long as you don't buy it. | Making fun of people who are different from you. |
| Ignoring your parent or teacher when that person asks you to do something. | Lying for someone who asked you to lie for him or her. |
| Downloading music or books off the Internet that are not intended to be free. | Doing whatever your parents or other family members do, even if it is wrong. |
| Answering someone with a lie because it's more interesting than the real answer. | Being mean to animals you don't like, even though they are no danger to you or others. |
| SMOKING WHEN NO ONE IS WATCHING. | |

# 2 Family Support and Communication

## SCHEDULE

| | | | |
|---|---|---|---|
| 9:00 a.m. | Registration | 12:45 p.m. | Break |
| 9:20 a.m. | Icebreaker | 1:05 p.m. | Rest |
| 9:35 a.m. | Introduction to retreat topic | 1:25 p.m. | Activity 6 |
| 9:40 a.m. | Activity 1 | 2:00 p.m. | Activity 7 |
| 10:00 a.m. | Juice break | 2:30 p.m. | Snack |
| 10:05 a.m. | Activity 2 | 2:45 p.m. | Activity 8 |
| 10:30 a.m. | Activity 3 | 3:30 p.m. | Clean up/Pack up |
| 10:45 a.m. | Activity 4 | 3:50 p.m. | Closing celebration |
| 11:15 a.m. | Activity 5 | 4:15 p.m. | Break |
| 11:40 a.m. | Lunch preparation | 4:30 p.m. | Parents pick up tweens |
| 12:00 noon | Lunch | | |

## Supplies

- NRSV Bibles
- retreat instructions and printed materials
- nametags or materials to make them
- easel pad or other large sheets of paper
- markers
- masking tape
- food service items: plates, cups, napkins, spoons

*(Note: Specific items for each activity are listed by activity.)*

## Food

**Midmorning break:**
- juice

**Lunch:**
- sandwich
- carrot sticks
- fruit
- chips
- ice cream
- drink

**Afternoon snack suggestions:**
- heart-shaped cookies
- bottled water

**Afternoon break:**
- lemonade

# 2 Family Support and Communication

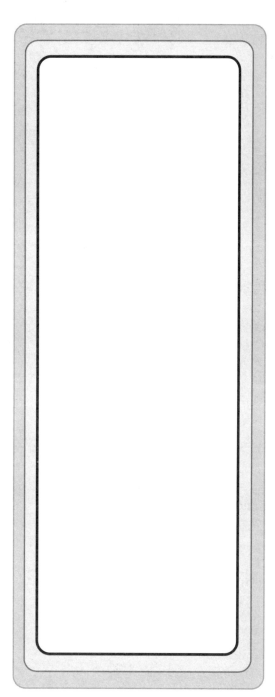

**FAITHPOINT:** Faith is born and nurtured in a strong family connection. Family relationships can give us a way to talk about God.

**SCRIPTURE:** Proverbs 15:4-5 and Proverbs 17:6

**SCRIPTURE REFLECTION:**

Proverbs 15:4-5 tells us that there is power in the way we speak—power to harm or to heal.

Proverbs 17:6 might be a way for children to consider how much their parents and perhaps grandparents value and love them. Help them think of ways that their parents and family care for and support them.

These attributes seem to be less and less true for many families in our society and may be a sensitive topic for young people. According to the Bible, it is the Christian parents' duty to provide their children with Christian learning and discipline. Discussions of family and marriage in the Bible are used to help us understand the way in which God is related to us. The parent figure, for some, is a secure and comforting presence or thought. For Jesus the term *father* seems to express an intimacy and tenderness that implies a deep relationship founded in love. This term, for some readers, helps draw the divine and the human elements of understanding, love, and family together.

For others it brings feelings of distrust, fear, deep sadness, or even trauma. The focus of this retreat is based on the assumption that the family lives of tweens are generally healthy as opposed to very dysfunctional. However, be prepared for a wide variety of responses, and watch for tweens who appear to be struggling with any activity because of emotional issues it may raise for them. The activities are designed to help the tweens explore how they can be in better relationship with their family for the benefit of all. Good, healthy relationships in the family most often lead to the tween growing up to become a healthy, responsible adult.

**PREPARATION:** See page 23 for the preparation check list.

# ICEBREAKER: SIBLINGS

Ask the participants to divide into groups that match their own family's sibling numbers. If a child is the only child in his or her family, that child will gather with others who are only children. If there are two children in their family, they gather with those who have two, and so forth.

If any groups are considerably larger than the others, divide them into smaller groupings for the next part of this exercise.

Give each group a piece of paper and a pen or pencil. Have each group discuss the positive qualities of their siblings and find four things they all have in common. Ask them to write the four shared positive qualities on their paper so they can report to the full group.

The group that has no siblings should talk about their own good qualities and find four they have in common.

After each group has reported its findings, give the tweens a few minutes to point out the qualities that seemed to be included in each group (if there are any).

**Say: An important part of getting along well in our families is knowing each person well and being able to find positive things about each person so that we can find the good things in family relationships. We have a tendency to focus more often on the negative instead of the positive. If we want the respect and support of our family members, we must also respect and support them. Knowing one another's positive traits helps us with these things.**

# ACTIVITY 1: GOOD TRADITIONS

When we think of family time together, we often think about the patterns and traditions that have developed through the years. There's comfort in telling someone, "In the summer my family goes on a lot of picnics down by the river." It brings out good memories and a good feeling about being with our family.

**Leader's Tip:** This is assuming the families of your tweens are functional and not abusive. You may need to adapt for other situations, so be aware of your tweens' family situations, if possible, before doing this exercise.

Give each group a set of the traditions cards, **Reproducible 2A**, and ask them to each pick out one tradition example card and think of a story or description to tell the others about that tradition from their own experience with their family.

## Siblings
**Supplies:**
- paper for each small group
- pen or pencil for each small group

**Preparation:**
- Gather supplies.

## Good Traditions
**Supplies:**
- Reproducible 2A, page 29
- scissors

**Preparation:**
- Photocopy Reproducible 2A and cut out the traditions cards, one set for each group of 4–5 youth.

## What Parents Provide

**Supplies:**
- paper
- pencils
- crayons, colored pencils, or fine-tip markers
- masking tape

**Preparation:**
- Gather supplies.

## Family Name Game

**Supplies:**
- beach ball for each circle of people

**Preparation:**
- Inflate the beach ball(s).

When they have selected cards and are ready, **say: What traditions, or family practices, do you feel good about? One at a time show your card to your small group and tell your story.**

## ACTIVITY 2: WHAT PARENTS PROVIDE

Give each tween a piece of 8½-by-11 paper and ask each one to draw two lines across the paper, dividing the sheet into three approximately equal parts. Then ask them to draw two more lines top to bottom, also dividing the sheet into three equal parts. This will give them nine boxes on their paper.

**Say: With crayons, colored pencils, or thin markers, draw a picture or write words in each box that symbolize some kind of support your parents provide for you** (*such as love, food, learning, and so forth*).

Have tweens put their papers on the wall or somewhere for everyone to see. They can see what support other tweens receive. This is a good reminder, especially for tweens who tend to be critical of their parents.

## ACTIVITY 3: FAMILY NAME GAME

Have the group form a circle. If your group is too large, form multiple circles.

The first person says the name of one of his or her family members and throws the ball to another person in the circle.

The person who catches the ball says the name of one family member and throws the ball to another person in the circle who hasn't yet had the ball.

Continue until the whole group has had a chance to catch and throw the ball.

Now, ask them to try to repeat throwing the ball in the same order as they did the first time.

Each time they throw the ball, they should use another family member's name. (Extended family members count.)

Continue to play for about five minutes, or until the group seems to be getting tired of playing.

## ACTIVITY 4: BIBLE STUDY
This activity will provide practice in looking up Scripture passages as the tweens focus on the discussion topic of families.

Have the entire group look up each passage as you work through the list below. For each Scripture **ask: What does this Scripture say that could apply to families?**

- Psalm 34:12-14
- Proverbs 12:18-19
- Galatians 6:9-10
- 1 Thessalonians 5:16-18
- 1 John 4:16b-17

## ACTIVITY 5: HOW WAS YOUR DAY?
Hand out copies of **Reproducible 2B** to four of the tweens. Have them act out the drama for the group.

Ask: What did the parents do or say that was helpful in this discussion? What was good about how the family interacted with one another?

## ACTIVITY 6: SMALL GROUPS
Divide into small groups for discussion.

Continue the discussion of the roleplay from Activity 5 with the questions on **Reproducible 2C**.

Before closing small groups, have each person write a prayer request on a 3-by-5 index card. Collect them to put in the "Family Affirmation Boxes."

### Bible Study
**Supplies:**
- Bibles

**Preparation:**
- none

### How Was Your Day?
**Supplies:**
- Reproducible 2B, page 30

**Preparation:**
- Make five photocopies of Reproducible 2B.

### Small Groups
**Supplies:**
- Reproducible 2C, page 31
- 3-by-5 index card for each person
- pen/pencil for each person

**Preparation:**
- Gather supplies.
- Photocopy Reproducible 2C, one per group.

## Family Affirmation Boxes

**Supplies:**
- Reproducible 2D, page 31
- small box for each tween (such as a shoebox)
- magazines with pictures
- scissors
- glue
- knife

**Preparation:**
- Gather supplies.
- Photocopy Reproducible 2D, one for each person.
- Cut a 1½- by 6-inch slit in the top of each box.

## Twister® With a Stretch

**Supplies:**
- Twister® game

**Preparation:**
- Acquire Twister® (box sets are inexpensive at toy stores). If the group is larger than one sheet can handle, either have multiple games or have tweens take turns.

## Closing Celebration

**Supplies:**
- Family Affirmation Boxes

**Preparation:**
- none

# ACTIVITY 7: FAMILY AFFIRMATION BOXES

Invite the tweens to cut and/or tear out magazine pictures and words that somehow represent good things about their family. Have them glue the magazine selections to cover their "Family Affirmation Boxes," being sure the boxes can be opened later.

Tweens should put their name on the bottom or end of their box. When done, set these aside to dry. These boxes are for each person to take home and explain to his or her parent(s). Give each tween a note to take home to his or her parent (**Reproducible 2D**).

# ACTIVITY 8: TWISTER® WITH A STRETCH

In this game, one person twirls the spinner and reads where the needle points to when it stops. Players move the designated foot or hand to the spot indicated on the spinner.

The difference for this game is that players must stretch to the farthest **color** they can reach with the correct hand or foot, without falling or touching other parts of their bodies to the sheet or ground. Each player is out when he or she makes an incorrect move, touches the ground, or falls to the ground. The last player is the "caller" for the next round.

**Say: Sometimes our lives get twisted up with problems, or being too busy, or having trouble in a class, or being irritated at a friend. We hope our families are places where we can sort things out and be supportive of one another.**

# CLOSING CELEBRATION

Ask the group to join in a circle.

Invite each tween to say one thing about his or her family for which that tween is thankful. Each person should hold up his or her "Family Affirmation Box" as the tweens offer thanks as a way of dedicating the boxes for their families to use together.

**Pray: God, we thank you for families who care and support one another. We ask for healing for families who have difficulty getting along, or who have problems that affect their relationships. Help us be more aware and interested in each person in our families so we can grow stronger. Teach us to be supportive of one another. We thank you that we are not alone in this world. Amen.**

| | |
|---|---|
| **WATCHING A FAVORITE MOVIE TOGETHER** | **ACHIEVEMENTS (LIKE GOOD GRADES)** |
| FAMILY VACATION TRIP | **CHRISTMAS EVE** |
| THANKSGIVING DAY | **CHRISTMAS MORNING** |
| FOURTH OF JULY | **SNOW OUTING** |
| **BIRTHDAYS** | **YOUR CHOICE (PICK YOUR OWN TRADITION)** |
| HARVEST OR HALLOWEEN | **YOUR CHOICE (PICK YOUR OWN TRADITION)** |

# How Was Your Day?

| Characters: | Scene: |
|---|---|
| Joe (tween), Mom, Dad, Charlotte (sister) | The family is at the dining table for a meal, having a discussion about what happened to a friend at school. |

**Dad:** So, how was your day?

**Joe:** I found out today that my friend Nicki had to stay after school yesterday in detention.

**Mom:** Do you know why she got detention?

**Dad:** Did she skip school or something?

**Charlotte:** I heard that she talked back to her science teacher and yelled at him in front of the class.

**Joe:** Yeah, that's what I heard too. But I don't know why she would do that when she knows she'll get in trouble.

**Dad:** How do you think the teacher felt about what happened?

**Joe:** I think he probably felt disrespected and angry. I sure would!

**Charlotte:** And he might have felt embarrassed about so many people hearing it too.

**Mom:** What would have been another way Nicki could have handled the problem more appropriately?

**Joe:** Maybe she could have asked to talk with the teacher after school. Or she could have asked her questions in a more polite way.

**Dad:** Do you think she deserved detention?

**Joe:** I really like Nicki, but I think what she did was wrong. So I guess she probably did.

**Charlotte:** If I ever get mad at a teacher, I think I'll find a better way to deal with it. Detention would be a real waste of time, and it would give my friends a bad impression of me.

**Joe:** Yeah, I hope she can talk to her parents about it and figure out how to deal with whatever's making her so angry. I think she needs some help. I wonder if she ever talks to her parents about things that are bugging her.

**Mom:** Maybe you'll get a chance to gently suggest that to her. I really think her parents would support her if they knew what she needed. I'm glad we had a chance to talk about this.

**Joe:** Yeah, me too.

# Talking With Parents

*Could this kind of conversation ever happen in your family?*

- Do you ever talk to your parent(s) about things that are happening in your life?

- Do you ever ask their advice?

- Do they listen to you when you talk to them?

- Do they ever offer ideas about how you could deal with situations or maybe with a person you don't get along with too well?

- If they offer advice, do you consider what they suggest? Would you?

- What are some other ways you receive support from your parents?

- Do your parents often do things to help you?

- What do you do to help your parents?

✂ - - - - - - - - - - - - - - - - - - - - - - - - - - - - - - - - - - -

Dear Parent:

At our retreat each tween decorated a box for his or her family.

You are encouraged to find a central location for this box and invite each family member to write affirmation notes to the family or prayers for the family to read.

We suggest you pick a time, once a week, when the family will open the box together and read what has been offered in the box. This is an opportunity for families to be supportive, complimentary, and encouraging of other family members, which we sometimes forget to do.

Notes may be as simple as "Great job on cleaning your room, _____ (*name*)!" or "Congratulations, Mom, on getting a raise at work."

Thank you.

# 3  Peaceful Solutions

## SCHEDULE

| | | | | |
|---|---|---|---|---|
| 9:00 a.m. | Registration | | 12:45 p.m. | Break |
| 9:20 a.m. | Icebreaker | | 1:05 p.m. | Rest |
| 9:35 a.m. | Introduction to retreat topic | | 1:25 p.m. | Activity 5 |
| 9:40 a.m. | Activity 1 | | 2:00 p.m. | Activity 6 |
| 10:00 a.m. | Juice break | | 2:30 p.m. | Snack and free time |
| 10:05 a.m. | Activity 2 | | 2:45 p.m. | Activity 7 |
| 10:30 a.m. | Activity 3 | | 3:30 p.m. | Clean up/Pack up |
| 11:00 a.m. | Activity 4 | | 4:00 p.m. | Closing celebration |
| 11:30 a.m. | Lunch preparation | | 4:15 p.m. | Break |
| 12:00 noon | Lunch | | 4:30 p.m. | Parents pick up tweens |

## Supplies

- NRSV Bibles
- retreat instructions and printed materials
- nametags or materials to make them
- easel pad or other large sheets of paper
- markers
- masking tape
- paper
- pens/pencils
- food service items: plates, cups, napkins, spoons

*(Note: Specific items for each activity are listed by activity.)*

## Food

**Mid-morning break:**
- juice

**Lunch:**
- sandwich
- carrot sticks
- fruit
- chips
- cookie
- drink

**Afternoon snack:**
- yogurt
- crackers
- cheese
- juice

**Afternoon break:**
- animal crackers
- bottled water

# 3  Peaceful Solutions

**FAITHPOINT:** Jesus teaches us to resolve our conflicts peacefully.

**SCRIPTURE:** Matthew 5:38-39 and Proverbs 12:18-19

**SCRIPTURE REFLECTION:**
We can choose to retaliate against those who hurt us, or we can, as Jesus teaches us, choose to respond nonviolently in a way that can transform relationships and communities. If someone tries to provoke us into reacting violently, we need to resist the temptation to fight back physically. It won't solve the problem, and it won't leave those involved with any other way to resolve their differences or understand one another better in the future.

We have power in the way we act and speak to harm or to heal.

**PREPARATION:**
See page 32 for the preparation check list.

**ICEBREAKER: TELL TWO THINGS**
Ask each person in turn to tell his or her name and two things he or she likes to do for fun. Go around the circle.

Ask the group if they learned anything new about anyone. Invite responses.

**ACTIVITY 1: WHY CONFLICTS?**
Ask: **What are some examples of where you have seen conflict arise, either personally or in our world?** (*Allow time for responses after each question.*) **Why do these conflicts arise? What are the various ways people handle conflict? What are some ways we can handle conflicts peacefully or nonviolently?**

## Tell Two Things
Supplies:
• none

Preparation:
• none

## Why Conflicts?
Supplies:
• none

Preparation:
• none

## Keeping the Peace

**Supplies:**
- Bible

**Preparation:**
- none

Say: The root of most conflicts is disrespect and/or disregard for other people's beliefs, actions, lifestyle, personality, or how they relate to others.

Say: Sometimes people are intent on retaliating for a previous offense by someone else. Sometimes people don't agree on decisions or processes. Sometimes people don't like someone else's behavior or lifestyle.

Ask: Are there appropriate reasons to treat others disrespectfully? (*no*) As people of God we must learn to relate to others in a loving, respectful way, regardless of what our feelings may urge us to do. We get to choose how to respond. Think about this as we go through this day together.

## ACTIVITY 2: KEEPING THE PEACE
Begin by reading this quotation to the group:

**Attitude and Choice**
The longer I live, the more I realize the impact of attitude on life. It is more important than the past, than education, than money, than circumstances, than failures, than successes, than what other people think or say or do. It is more important than appearance, giftedness or skill.

It will make or break a company . . . a church . . . a home. The remarkable thing is we have a choice every day regarding the attitude we will embrace for that day. We cannot change our past. . . . We cannot change the fact that people will act in a certain way. We cannot change the inevitable. The only thing we can do is play on the one string we have, and that is our attitude. . . .

I am convinced that life is 10% what happens to me and 90% how I react to it. And so it is with you . . . we are in charge of our attitudes. (Charles R. Swindoll)

Ask: Can you think of some instances at your school or in your neighborhood when you reacted to something that happened, rather than taking time to think and making a more appropriate response?

Invite responses and stories, and follow up each one with the question, "What do you wish you had done or said instead?"

Say: We usually cannot actually change people or circumstances, but we can change our own attitudes and choices. If we learn to do this well, we can avoid what might otherwise turn into a conflict or at least a misunderstanding or hurt feelings.

Say: As Christian peacemakers, we may feel we have an additional responsibility in the face of conflict. Instead of just standing by and watching someone cause trouble, why not say something to encourage that person to stop?

Ask: What might the consequences be? Could it still be worth intervening to help someone else?

Invite open discussion.

Leader's Tip: You may need to start the discussion by giving a specific instance, such as bullying in school.

Close by reading Proverbs 10:10.

## ACTIVITY 3: FINGERPAINTING

Say: Try painting a picture where the colors stay vivid, without turning to brown. Use the theme of peace and nonviolence to inspire you.

Allow twenty minutes for painting.

Say: You may have discovered that when you go over the lines, you sometimes get brown paint, or at least something different from what you originally had. This is representative of when we disrespect one another's boundaries; one another's space; one another's stuff; one another's ideas; and one another's feelings. It changes things, and it might even get ugly.

Invite the tweens to display their pictures, clean up their work space, and wash their hands.

## Fingerpainting
**Supplies:**
- fingerpaints
- fingerpainting paper (slick)
- newspapers to cover table
- soap and water for cleanup

**Preparation:**
- Cover tables with paper for protection.
- Gather supplies.

## Journaling

**Supplies:**
- journal (or writing paper) for each person
- pens or pencils

**Preparation:**
- Gather supplies.

## ACTIVITY 4: JOURNALING

**Say: If we have done something wrong and need to be forgiven, most of us know it, but we don't always know how to ask for forgiveness. There are several steps to receiving forgiveness. I am going to give you these steps, and after I describe each one, I would like you to write in your journal** (*or on your paper*) **the key words and perhaps another thought you have about that.**

Review with your tweens some steps involved in being forgiven.

- Prayer: Put the problem in God's hands. Pray about it.

**Say: Write about this in your journal.** (*Give time for writing.*)

- Sincerity: Be, and practice being, truly sorry.

**Say: If we have done something we shouldn't have done, we should feel sorry. Be able to say, "I'm sorry." Write about this in your journal.** (*Give time for writing.*)

- Repent.

**Say: Admit you are wrong. Be able to say, "I was wrong." Quit denying you did it (or neglected to do it). Write about this in your journal.** (*Give time for writing.*)

- Act in a way that conveys your new attitude or choice of behavior. Take intentional steps to get along better with others or to be kinder.

**Say: Write about this in your journal.** (*Give time for writing.*) **There are also times when we need to forgive others. There are steps we can take for that too. Let's continue in our journals. Steps for forgiving are these:**

- Prayer: Put the problem in God's hands. Pray about it.

**Say: Write about this in your journal.** (*Give time for writing.*)

- Sympathy: Think about why the person did what he or she did.

**Say: Maybe you'll be able to figure it out. And maybe you'll understand what happened. Write about this in your journal.** (*Give time for writing.*)

- Sincerity: Really mean it when you say, "I'm sorry." Try to remember the good things about the person you are asking to forgive you.

**Say: Write about this in your journal.** (*Give time for writing.*)

## ACTIVITY 5: PARAPHRASING

Divide the participants into two groups. Hand out one piece of paper and one pen or pencil to each group. Post the quotations on the wall.

Assign each group one of the quotations.

Ask them to write a paraphrase of their quotation.

Remind them that a paraphrase is restating the meaning of the phrase in your own words—different from the original phrase.

Give them five minutes to work on these.

Ask each group to read their quotation to the group and then read their paraphrase. Invite the other group to cheer for each group after they read.

## ACTIVITY 6: WINK 'EM GAME

Players are arranged in a circle on the floor, in partners, with one squatting and one guard kneeling behind the squatting person. One guard is "It" and has no one in front of him or her. That person winks, as subtly as possible, at one of the squatting persons in the circle. If the squatter sees the wink, the squatter darts forward and tries to get to the open space in front of the winker before the guard can prevent it by placing his or her hands on the squatter's shoulders. Guards must keep their hands by their sides except when they are reaching for their squatter's shoulders as they try to get away.

**Leader's Tip:** This can also be played in chairs instead of squatting, if you prefer.

Play about fifteen minutes, or longer if the group is enjoying the game.

### Paraphrasing
**Supplies:**
- large paper for quotations
- marker
- paper, one piece per group
- pen/pencil, one per group

**Preparation:**
- Write each quotation below in a large "bubble" or word balloon (like in the comic strips).

**Quotations:**
If we have no peace, it is because we have forgotten that we belong to each other. —Mother Teresa

The best way to destroy an enemy is to make him a friend. —Abraham Lincoln

### Wink 'Em Game
**Supplies:**
- optional: chairs (one for every two people playing)

**Preparation:**
- optional: Place chairs in a circle.

### Group Pledge

**Supplies:**
- Reproducible 3A, page 39
- pen

**Preparation:**
- Fill in the name of your group on the "Pledge of Nonviolence" on Reproducible 3A.
- Photocopy Reproducible 3A for each person.

### Closing Celebration

**Supplies:**
- "Pledge of Nonviolence"

**Preparation:**
- none

## ACTIVITY 7: GROUP PLEDGE

Fill in the name of your tween group on the "Pledge of Nonviolence," **Reproducible 3A**. Then this pledge should be copied for each person.

Introduce the "Pledge of Nonviolence" by reading each item. Invite discussion on each one.

Explain that by making this pledge, they are stating their intention to live a more thoughtful life. Have tweens fold their pledge, accordion style, to fit easily into a wallet or pocket as a reminder of their commitment to nonviolence. Urge them to share the pledge with their family and friends. Encourage them to use it as a guideline for how they can live more peacefully in the future.

## CLOSING CELEBRATION

- Have the group stand in a circle.

- Ask for a volunteer to read each section of the "Pledge of Nonviolence."

- After the last paragraph, have the whole group say aloud together: "This is our pledge. We will check ourselves monthly to keep our promise to build a more peaceable tween group."

**Pray: God, we pledge ourselves to you. You have heard our intentions to live as peaceful people. You know our hearts. Help us live up to the pledge we have made so our world will be a better place, one tween group at a time. Be with us as we leave this place, and don't let us forget what we have learned together today. Amen.**

**Leader's Tip:** Do not say that you will be checking up monthly unless you intend to follow through.

# Pledge of Nonviolence

As members of _____, we make a commitment to try to live more peacefully. We want to help eliminate violence by making a pledge to:

**Think Before Acting**
When I become frustrated or angry with others, I will try to take a moment to think about my best response, rather than fighting back verbally or physically. I will avoid using words and actions that hurt others or that are self-destructive.

**Listen More Carefully**
I will make a better effort to hear what others are saying, and I will try to understand what they mean and how they feel, whether or not I agree with them.

**Make Apologies**
When I have said or done something that hurts another's feelings, I will try to make a sincere apology to that person and heal the feelings of hurt or anger between us.

**Be Forgiving**
Instead of carrying a grudge and remaining angry or disappointed with others, I will try to let go of the feelings that keep me from putting what has happened behind me.

**Respect All**
I will be more careful to treat all living things with respect and to help care for our natural environment, as well as for persons in need.

**Be a Problem Solver**
When our group has a problem, I will work with others to resolve the issue in a respectful manner that honors the group members.

**Make and Encourage Nonviolent Choices**
I will try to help create a more peaceful society by avoiding things that glorify violence, especially when making choices about what I watch or listen to, as a show of my pledge to nonviolence; and I will try to encourage others to do the same.

**Stand for Peace**
When I encounter any form of violence at school, in our group, at home, or anywhere else, I will stand up for finding peaceful resolutions and for the fair treatment of every person, and I will resist the poor behavior of others around me.

**Great Tween Getaways**

# 4 A Passionate Heart

---

## SCHEDULE

| | | | | |
|---|---|---|---|---|
| 9:00 a.m. | Registration | | 12:45 p.m. | Break |
| 9:20 a.m. | Icebreaker | | 1:05 p.m. | Rest |
| 9:35 a.m. | Introduction to retreat topic | | 1:25 p.m. | Activity 5 |
| 9:40 a.m. | Activity 1 | | 2:00 p.m. | Activity 6 |
| 10:00 a.m. | Juice break | | 2:30 p.m. | Snack |
| 10:05 a.m. | Activity 2 | | 2:45 p.m. | Activity 7 |
| 10:30 a.m. | Activity 3 | | 3:30 p.m. | Clean up/Pack up |
| 11:00 a.m. | Activity 4 | | 4:00 p.m. | Closing celebration |
| 11:30 a.m. | Lunch preparation | | 4:15 p.m. | Break |
| 12:00 noon | Lunch | | 4:30 p.m. | Parents pick up tweens |

---

## Supplies

- NRSV Bibles
- retreat instructions and printed materials
- nametags or materials to make them
- easel pad or other large sheets of paper
- markers
- masking tape
- paper for each person
- pen for each person
- food service items: plates, cups, napkins, spoons

*(Note: Specific items for each activity are listed by activity.)*

---

## Food

**Mid-morning break:**
- juice

**Lunch:**
- pocket bread sandwich
- carrot sticks
- fruit
- chips
- cookie

**Afternoon snack:**
- lemonade
- cheese and crackers

**Afternoon break:**
- lemonade

# 4   A Passionate Heart

**FAITHPOINT**: Our faith helps us to live lives full of meaning and experiences that give our lives purpose.

**SCRIPTURE**: Micah 6:8 and John 10:10b

**SCRIPTURE REFLECTION**:
It is clear from these Scriptures that life is meant not just to "be," but to be filled with meaning and experiences that give us purpose. Tweens often see their lives as just individual days. It is up to the adults who work with them to help them see beyond the day to day, to help them develop Christian values, and to help them learn to care about something besides themselves. Learning to have a passion for making life better for others will also bring them joy and depth in their own lives.

**PREPARATION**:
See page 40 for the preparation check list.

**ICEBREAKER: WHAT'S YOUR PASSION?**
Say: One of the definitions of *passion* is "boundless enthusiasm" for something. It could be a sport you play, music, a favorite game, creating art, a specific skill you have acquired or are working toward, spending time with your friends, or serving other people. The possibilities are nearly endless. As we gain more and more experiences and knowledge in our lives, we begin to sort out what we are curious about, what we are truly interested in, and eventually, what we really have a passion for—what tugs on our hearts.

Say: God gives us hearts that can fill with a passion to make a difference, or that can fill with compassion for others. When we realize this and begin to discover what our passions are, we also benefit from the experiences we give to others.

## What's Your Passion?

Supplies:
• none

Preparation:
• none

### Acrostics

**Supplies:**
- Bible
- large sheet of paper for each group
- marker(s) for each group

**Preparation:**
- Print words below on large sheets of paper, one word per sheet.

```
F       G       E
R       E       N
E       N       R
E       E       I
L       R       C
Y       O       H
        U       E
        S       D
```

Ask: What do you have a passion for? Turn to a person near you and get into pairs. Ask your partner these two questions: "What do you have a passion for or care deeply about?" and "What makes your life meaningful?"

Allow several minutes for these conversations. Also realize that many may not be able to come up with answers for these questions. Be prepared to give an example from your own life, if they should ask what you mean.

Tell them when their time is up. Ask them how many were able to answer the questions. Acknowledge that it is okay to not have an answer yet.

## ACTIVITY 1: ACROSTICS

Read Proverbs 11:24-25 to the participants (or ask for a volunteer to read the verses).

Divide the participants into small groups.

Assign each group one of these words: *freely, generous, enriched.* Write each word vertically down the side of a separate large sheet of paper.

**Leader's Tip:** If your group is large, feel free to have multiple groups with the same words, or add your own words from the Scripture.

Ask each group to create a definition of their word and create an acrostic (see definition below) of their assigned word.

When they are ready, ask each group to share their word definition and acrostic with the full group.

An *acrostic* is a series of words in which the first letter of each word is used to form a word, name, or message when read in sequence. You are giving tweens the first letter of each word by giving them one of the three designated words listed above. If their word were *hope*, they would make a series of words with the first word starting with the letter *h*, the second word starting with the letter *o*, and so forth. For example, *HOPE* could be *Helping Other People Everywhere*. (The words do not have to make a sentence.) The series of words does not have to relate to the meaning of the original word, although if they can find words that relate, it is a stronger exercise. The series of words should be only positive words (avoiding sarcasm and negative or offensive words).

## ACTIVITY 2: DO YOU HAVE IT?

**Leader's Tip:** If you know the song and have the ability, begin this activity by singing "I've Got the Joy."

Read John 10:10b.

Hand out the "Do You Have It?" worksheet, **Reproducible 4A**. Ask tweens to find their own space away from others and fill in the statements. Allow at least ten minutes.

When everyone has completed the worksheets, ask tweens to gather in groups of three or four with an adult in each group, if possible.

Ask them to each pick five statements to share with their group.

## ACTIVITY 3: AMOEBA TAG

**Say:** We know that life isn't just fun and games. But we also know that a good balance between working, learning, playing, praying, resting, and more is important to a well-rounded and happy life. So we're going to play a game of "Amoeba Tag."

Review the instructions with the tweens so everyone will play the game the same way:

Two people are "It."

They hold hands and chase the other people.

The person they catch joins the chain by linking hands. When another person is caught, they can stay together or split two and two.

They must split by even numbers and can link together at will. The same people remain "It," even though they may have split from each other. This game is played until no one is left alone.

Play the game.

If there is time, begin another game by assigning two new people to play "It." Play for fifteen minutes before you gather together.

### Do You Have It?
**Supplies:**
- Bible
- pencils or pens
- Reproducible 4A, page 47

**Preparation:**
- Photocopy Reproducible 4A, one for each person.

### Amoeba Tag
**Supplies:**
- none

**Preparation:**
- none

## Loving Kindness

**Supplies:**
- easel pad or large sheet of paper
- marker

**Preparation:**
- none

**Ask: What are some similarities between this game and real life?** (*If everyone is reluctant to share, give suggestions such as: Sometimes we're alone. Sometimes we have others to hold on to. There can be safety in numbers. Sometimes we get pulled along with the crowd. Sometimes life is fast, and sometimes it gets bogged down. Sometimes we just have a lot of fun.*)

At this point give the tweens a fifteen-minute break and encourage them to get something to drink.

## ACTIVITY 4: LOVING KINDNESS

**Say: This is going to be a brainstorming session. The rules for brainstorming are as follows:**

- **No evaluating of ideas.**
- **All ideas are good—no negative comments.**
- **Think big.**
- **Speak one at a time.**
- **Try starting your idea by saying, "Yes, and . . ."**

**Say: Our brainstorm topic is "Loving Kindness." We are looking for ways to show kindness, caring, and respect for others. This includes people we know and people we don't know.**

**Leader's Tip:** Some of these ideas could get developed into a "Random Acts of Kindness" outing at a later date.

Make a list as ideas are given.

If tweens have trouble giving ideas, you could offer a few suggestions, such as:

- Hold a door for someone at a store.
- Reach an item on a store shelf for someone with mobility difficulties.
- Compliment someone.
- Ask to mow or rake your neighbor's yard for free.

## ACTIVITY 5: MINGLE AND MATCH

Say: Part of what makes our lives meaningful is relating to other people. It is fun to find others who have the same likes, dislikes, dreams, and interests that we have. So here's a chance to find out more about our group.

Give the tweens these instructions:

- Everyone needs to stand in the middle of the room fairly close together.
- When I yell "Mingle," you will all start walking around among one another, saying, "Mingle, mingle, mingle . . ." until I yell "Match." When you hear "Match," stop and turn to a partner next to you. Make sure everyone has a partner.
- Talk with your partner to find something you both have in common.
- When I yell "Mingle," you will mingle again, and find a new partner when I yell "Match," and so forth.
- Each time try to find a different activity in common, even though it's with a new partner.

Continue until most people have talked to most of the others, or do this activity for a timed period.

Ask the group to share some of the more unusual things they discovered in common with someone.

## ACTIVITY 6: SMALL GROUPS

Divide tweens into small groups of three or four and discuss the tough questions below. Read the questions one at a time, giving a couple of minutes to discuss each. Adults will probably need to assist them in these conversations. Allow fifteen to twenty minutes for discussion.

**Tough Questions:**
- How does being a follower of God make your life more meaningful?
- God helps us discern or discover what we can do to make a difference in our world. For whom can we possibly make a difference? (*friends, families, community, country/world*) In what ways?
- How do you feel when you've done something nice or helpful for another person and he or she benefits from what you've done? You may be the only person who has done something for that person that day!

### Mingle and Match
**Supplies:**
- none

**Preparation:**
- none

### Small Groups
**Supplies:**
- optional: easel pad or large sheet of paper
- optional: marker

**Preparation:**
- optional: Write out the discussion questions listed at left.

## Prayer Balloons

**Supplies:**
- balloons
- paper
- pens
- scissors

**Preparation:**
- Cut paper into little strips.
- Gather supplies.

## Closing Celebration

**Supplies:**
- balloons from previous activity

**Preparation:**
- none

## ACTIVITY 7: PRAYER BALLOONS

Give each tween a pen and a small slip of paper.

Say: Write your answer to this question on your little slip of paper: "What major needs in the world would you like to help solve or ease?"

Give each tween a balloon.

Say: Fold up your slip of paper as tiny as possible. Insert your paper into your balloon. Blow up your balloon and tie off the end. Hold on to your balloon and wait for others to finish.

## CLOSING CELEBRATION

Get into a tight group and have everyone toss his or her balloon in the air. Try to keep all the balloons up in the air without dropping to the floor or breaking for as long as possible.

When a balloon drops or pops, begin again and try to keep the balloons in the air longer than the previous try. After several tries, have everyone hold on to a balloon (any balloon—not likely his or her own).

Say: If any one of us tried to keep these balloons in the air by ourselves, we couldn't manage more than a few at the most. But when we all work together to keep them in the air, we can do so much more, both in number and in length of time. Some of the world's problems seem way beyond our ability to help and to make a difference, but together we can do things that aren't possible separately. God brings us together, and we can make a difference.

Say: One at a time I'm going to ask you to pop the balloon you are holding. When your balloon breaks, find the slip of paper and read it to the group.

Pray: God, we want to make a difference. We want to find a deeper purpose and meaning for our lives, and we want to do that through you. Help us see the needs of the world and strive to find ways to make life better for others. Keep reminding us that we are your hands and feet on this earth. Keep reminding us that together we can do so much more than apart. Keep reminding us to have a heart for passion, for caring about more than ourselves. Amen.

# Do You Have It?

*What makes you happy? What brings you joy? Complete the sentences below.*

For me, to be happy means I _____

_____

I really enjoy _____

_____

I am happiest when I'm _____

_____

My favorite thing to do alone is _____

_____

My favorite thing to do with my family is _____

_____

I enjoy my friends most when we're _____

_____

I feel a good sense of accomplishment when _____

_____

I feel like I am making a difference when _____

_____

I like to make others happy by _____

_____

My life is important because _____

_____

# 5 Doing Justice: A Service Retreat

## SCHEDULE

| | | | |
|---|---|---|---|
| 9:00 a.m. | Registration | 2:30 p.m. | Activity 4 |
| 9:20 a.m. | Icebreaker | 2:45 p.m. | Snack |
| 9:35 a.m. | Introduction to retreat topic | 3:00 p.m. | Activity 5 |
| 9:40 a.m. | Activity 1 | 4:00 p.m. | Clean up/Pack up |
| 10:00 a.m. | Juice break | 4:15 p.m. | Closing celebration |
| 10:05 a.m. | Activity 2 | 4:25 p.m. | Break |
| 10:30 a.m. | Gather to prepare for hunger project (take sack lunches) | 4:30 p.m. | Parents pick up tweens |
| 10:45 a.m. | Explain project and load to leave for work site/area (Activity 3) | | |
| 1:45 p.m. | Arrive back at retreat site | | |
| 2:00 p.m. | Rest time | | |

*Times might have to be adjusted to accommodate travel time.*

## Supplies

- NRSV Bibles
- retreat instructions and printed materials
- nametags or materials to make them
- easel pad or other large sheets of paper
- markers
- masking tape
- paper for each person
- pen for each person
- food service items: plates, cups, napkins, spoons

*(Note: Specific items for each activity are listed by activity.)*

## Food

**Lunch:**
- whatever meal is served at the service project, or sack lunches including sandwich, veggie sticks, chips, cookie, and drink.

**Afternoon break:**
- drink such as lemonade
- light snack such as popcorn or fruit

# 5 Doing Justice: A Service Retreat

**FAITHPOINT:** As disciples of Christ we must commit ourselves to living faithfully and doing justice.

**SCRIPTURE:** Luke 4:16-19

**SCRIPTURE REFLECTION:**
Jesus' life and ministry give us the model of how God intends for us to live our lives. This Scripture essentially describes a purpose statement for life. It describes a life of service and care for others and a selfless approach to finding meaning through living the faithful life. Helping young people understand the value of a life that isn't "all about me" will help shape their approach to life and will help them intentionally take action to better their community and world.

**PREPARATION:**
See page 48 for the preparation check list.

The location of this retreat will need to be determined by the location of your hunger service project. Find agencies in your area that serve a lunch meal for hungry persons in your community. Arrange with one of them to have your retreat group assist with serving and/or preparing at least a portion of the meal. If they are hesitant because of the younger age level of the tweens involved, perhaps they would welcome having your tweens bake cookies or hand out fresh fruit—whatever they are comfortable with. Be sure they know the age range of the tweens and the number of people you will be bringing.

You may even need to divide into two or three groups if there are too many to serve in the settings available.

Determine the travel time and transportation needed and adjust the retreat schedule accordingly.

Either arrange for your group to have lunch at the agency you are working with or pack sack lunches to take with you to eat afterwards. Have adequate adult supervision and prepare tweens for working in small work groups. Assign buddies (within each small work group) so they can help keep track of each other for safety purposes.

Prepare and print discussion questions for the small groups (Activity 4) following the service project.

### Favorite Things

**Supplies:**
- paper
- pen

**Preparation:**
- Make a list of small work groups for the day.

### Sent by God

**Supplies:**
- Bible

**Preparation:**
- none

### Color Puzzles

**Supplies:**
- Bible
- puzzles you make
- envelopes
- scissors
- colored paper
- pen

**Preparation:**
- Make puzzle pieces and place each set in an envelope.

**Leader's Tip:** If you are familiar with the song "We Are a Rainbow," you might wish to open this activity by singing it.

## ICEBREAKER: FAVORITE THINGS

Divide tweens into the work groups they will be in later in the day.

Have them share:
- Their favorite thing to do to help out at home.
- Their best work skill (adults may have to help them with this one).
- What they are expecting to see today at the service project.

## ACTIVITY 1: SENT BY GOD

Read Isaiah 42:6-9.

**Say: Just as Isaiah speaks of being called to serve God, we are also called to serve God. In our own lives we have opportunities to serve God by serving God's people who are in need.**

Read 1 Timothy 4:12.

**Say: Instead of being a follower, be an example and a leader for others to follow, as you follow Jesus.**

Ask how these ideas will apply to the service project today.

## ACTIVITY 2: COLOR PUZZLES

Read John 13:34-35 and Galatians 3:26-29 as a reminder that we are all children of God and part of a community of faith.

This exercise requires cooperation and communication. It will give tweens an opportunity to work together to solve puzzles in a cooperative manner and will reveal how they work with others. This can be the catalyst for discussion about the service project the group will be doing today. Following instructions and cooperating with one another will be important to the success of the service project.

Divide tweens into groups of three persons each. Give each small group an envelope with puzzle pieces. (Each envelope should contain a piece of colored paper cut into the same number of odd-shaped puzzle pieces. Each envelope's puzzle pieces should be a different color from those of all other envelopes, but should be cut identically so the pieces are interchangeable. The easiest way to do this is to use a pencil to draw your puzzle pieces onto a sheet of paper. Photocopy the paper using different-colored papers to make several puzzles, then cut them apart. Any puzzle shapes will do.)

**Say: The object of this game is for each small group to create one complete puzzle, with each piece being a different color.**

This means the small color groups are going to have to share their pieces with the other color groups. You will need to adapt the number of puzzle pieces to the number of groups, and each group's puzzle needs to be a different color.

Instructions for the participants (give each at the appropriate time):

- **First five minutes:** You cannot talk. You may offer one of your pieces of the puzzle to another group, but you cannot ask, verbally or with gestures, for a piece you need, and you cannot take pieces from others.

- **Next five minutes:** You cannot talk, but you may use gestures to indicate your need for other puzzle pieces. The owners of the piece may offer the piece to you, if they wish. You cannot take it yourself.

- **Next five minutes:** You can now talk in order to complete your puzzles, if you haven't already finished.

- Gather back into your full group and ask participants to share some of what they experienced during the game by discussing the following questions.

**Ask: Did the other color groups willingly share their pieces? Did some obstruct your progress by withholding pieces? Were some color groups more cooperative than others? What does this exercise tell you about how this retreat group works together?**

## ACTIVITY 3: HUNGER SERVICE PROJECT
Either before leaving for the project site, or while traveling, if you are all together on a bus, cover the following:

- Describe the project you have selected for the group and explain what the agency does for the people in need.

- Explain the role of this retreat group in assisting the agency.

## Hunger Service Project
**Supplies:**
- to be determined by project
- permission slips

**Preparation:**
- Select a project.
- Contact the agency to find out its needs and to make arrangements for group activity at the agency.
- Send home permission slips to have them signed by parents. They must be returned and in hand before leaving for the project (see p. 96).
- Recruit drivers and helpers.
- Make arrangements for the noon meal.

### Small Groups
**Supplies:**
- Reproducible 5A, page 55

**Preparation:**
- Photocopy Reproducible 5A, one for each group.

### Planning Your Future Service Project
**Supplies:**
- easel pad or other large sheets of paper
- marker

**Preparation:**
- none

---

- Give tweens their work group assignment so they know who they will be working with and what adult is responsible for them.

- Give each tween his or her buddy assignment and explain that buddies are supposed to keep track of each other during this project.

When you have arrived at the project site, have tweens get out of the vehicle(s) and gather in their work groups. Remind them that they are to stay with their group the entire time, unless you tell them differently once work begins.

Meet the agency staff and get directions.

Complete the project.

When tweens have finished, ask each work group to return to the vehicles for the return trip to the retreat site.

If they have not already eaten lunch and have sack lunches, you may want them to eat in the vehicle before leaving (or at a nearby park or church lawn, if the weather is good).

Return to the retreat site.

Participants should use rest rooms as needed and gather for a fifteen-minute rest time.

## ACTIVITY 4: SMALL GROUPS
Have the full group meet and divide into small discussion groups different from their work groups. Give each group a copy of the discussion questions on **Reproducible 5A** and invite them to reflect on their experiences that day.

## ACTIVITY 5: PLANNING YOUR FUTURE SERVICE PROJECT
Have someone record the answers to the questions on the following page, perhaps by writing on an easel pad or other large sheets of paper for the group to see. Be sure to save these for later use in making arrangements for the next service project.

Say: **Today we served other people by** (what you did on your project). **We would like to create another opportunity to serve in the future. Here are some questions to help us determine what kind of service that might be:**

- Why is it a good idea to take time to help other people with something they need?

- What kinds of situations might people be in where they would need some help?

- Are there people in our congregation who need assistance of some kind?

- Are there tweens in our neighborhood who need something we could provide?

- If we wanted to provide food for people, what are some ways we could do that? *(making and distributing sack lunches to people who are homeless; providing a meal at our church and inviting the neighborhood; serving a meal at an agency or shelter; organizing a canned/boxed food drive to gather food for a food bank or specific agency who can appropriately distribute it; and so forth)*

- If we wanted to provide blankets or sleeping bags for people, what are some ways we could do that?

- If we wanted to provide books for children who are living in poverty, what are some ways we could do that?

- If we wanted to provide yard work for someone unable to do his or her own, what are some ways we could do that?

- What are the skills we have that could be used to help other people?

- Which of the types of service we have talked about in this session are of the most interest to you? (*You might want to do a show of hands for each type.*)

- Which of these types of service are we most capable of doing well?

- Where do we think might be the greatest need in our city?

- What type of project would you like to do next? (*You might want to have a show of hands for each type.*)

- What steps might be involved in doing this project? (*Make a list.*)

## Closing Celebration

**Supplies:**
- none

**Preparation:**
- none

## CLOSING CELEBRATION

Say: When it comes to justice, one of the hardest things to realize might be that we can make a difference by making informed choices. If we know that a certain brand of food is produced by people who are paid far less than is fair, we might choose not to buy that brand of food until the problem is resolved. If enough people choose not to buy that brand, the company will get the message that underpaying their workers is not acceptable to the people wanting the product.

Say: We know there is enough food in the world for all people, but we also know that the food is not equally distributed so that each person has access to a fair share of the available food. So many starve while others throw away leftover food.

Ask the children to think about other examples of injustice.

Pray: Loving God, we are learning about how fortunate we are to have been born in the places and times we were born. We know that we have access to more than our share of every good thing in life. Help us seek ways to do justice in our world. Don't let us forget the people we served today and their needs. Don't let us forget those whose needs are not being met. Thank you for the privilege and opportunity to serve others in Jesus' name. Amen.

# Reflection Questions

How do you feel about your experiences today?

What surprised you about the people you met today?

Did you notice any sounds or smells that you don't usually experience?

What did you learn today?

Did you learn the names of any people we served today? Who are they?

What is something you would like for yourself? What do you want?

What is something you want for the people you met today?

Are the answers to the last two questions similar or different? Why or why not?

What can you, and possibly your family, do to serve others in the future?

**Great Tween Getaways**

# Overnight RETREATS

The retreat schedules show how to fit various items into the day. The actual length of any one activity can vary greatly from group to group. You are encouraged to adjust the schedule to fit your group's needs.

It will also be important to allow free time between some activities, especially with this age level. Their attention span is limited, so many activities will tend to go more quickly than expected.

Come prepared to have additional appropriate things for tweens to do during free time. This can be good group-building time simply by having them spend extended time together.

It is also important to have sufficient rest time. Don't forget to provide lots of water. Developing bodies and brains need it!

# **6** Being a Positive Influence

---

## SCHEDULE

**First Evening**

| | |
|---|---|
| 6:30 p.m. | Gather to carpool to location, if off-site |
| 7:00 p.m. | Leave for retreat destination |
| Arrive on site | Get settled into sleeping areas (get beds ready and pajamas out) |
| | Gather and put on nametags, if it's a large group or they do not know one another well |
| | Give tour of facility, if needed |
| | Go through rules |
| | Set up buddies |
| | Introduce retreat theme |
| 9:00 p.m. | Icebreaker |
| 9:15 p.m. | Activity 1 |
| 9:30 p.m. | Get ready for bed (pajamas on and sitting on bed by 9:50) |
| 9:50 p.m. | Bedtime story (either from your own experience or a short one that you read) |
| 10:00 p.m. | Lights out and quiet |

**Full Day**

| | |
|---|---|
| 7:15 a.m. | Wake up, get dressed and ready for the day |
| 7:45 a.m. | Breakfast set-up |
| 8:00 a.m. | Breakfast |
| 8:30 a.m. | Announcements and cleanup |
| 9:15 a.m. | Morning watch (including Scripture, singing, prayer) |
| 9:30 a.m. | Reminder of retreat theme topic |
| 9:35 a.m. | Activity 2 |
| 10:00 a.m. | 5-minute juice break |
| 10:05 a.m. | Activity 3 |
| 10:30 a.m. | Physical game |
| 10:45 a.m. | Activity 4 |
| 11:15 a.m. | Small group activity |
| 11:30 a.m. | Lunch preparation |
| 12:00 noon | Lunch |
| 12:45 p.m. | Break |
| 1:05 p.m. | Rest |
| 1:25 p.m. | Activity 5 |
| 2:00 p.m. | Activity 6 |
| 2:30 p.m. | Snack |
| 2:45 p.m. | Activity 7 |
| 3:30 p.m. | Clean up/Pack up |
| 3:50 p.m. | Closing celebration |
| 4:15 p.m. | Depart for return to church |
| ____ p.m. | Parents pick up youth |

---

## **Supplies**

- several translations of the Bible
- retreat instructions and printed materials
- nametags or materials to make them
- easel pad or other large sheets of paper
- old newspapers
- markers
- masking tape
- paper for each person
- pen for each person
- food service items: plates, cups, napkins, spoons

(*Note:* Specific items for each activity are listed by activity.)

## **Food**

- Snack for Friday night
- Saturday breakfast
- Saturday lunch
- Saturday afternoon snack

(*Note:* Keep plenty of bottled water on hand. Brains need lots of water.)

# 6 Being a Positive Influence

**FAITHPOINT**: As disciples of Christ we are called to have the courage to be a model of Christian love to our friends.

**SCRIPTURE**: 1 Corinthians 16:13-14 and Proverbs 12:26

## SCRIPTURE REFLECTION:

As Christians we are called to live with integrity, honesty, and kindness. Being courageous may mean standing up for someone who is being picked on in the lunchroom. It also means staying true to who you are and who God calls you to be. When tweens choose friends who have similar values, they can remain good examples for one another. They tend to choose behaviors that their friends would agree with or approve of. The people who tweens hang with in their remaining school years may determine the kind of adults they become.

## PREPARATION:

See page 58 for the preparation check list.

## ICEBREAKER: IF YOU . . .

Every person needs to sit on a chair, in a circle facing inward. Explain that you will give specific instructions. Begin by saying, "If you . . . (*fill in one of the items from the list below*), move (*choose a number*) chairs to your (*right or left—you choose which direction*). They must sit individually on that chair or together on that chair. They might easily end up with three or four people on some chairs—some having to sit in the laps of others.

- are wearing socks right now . . .
- have blue eyes . . .
- have clothes on your bedroom floor . . .
- have ever baked a cake . . .
- like to swim . . .
- have ever flown a kite . . .
- have ever been to Canada . . .
- wear shoes size five or smaller . . .
- have a picture of a friend with you at this retreat . . .
- play the piano . . .
- have a pet at home . . .

(continued on p. 60)

## If You . . .

**Supplies:**
- chairs

**Preparation:**
- none

- read your Bible at least twice a week . . .
- have a hobby . . .
- are the youngest child in your family . . .
- help with housework at home . . .
- like riding roller coasters . . .
- have ever built a sand castle . . .
- are sitting on someone's lap . . .

**Ask: What are some things many of you seem to have in common?**

## ACTIVITY 1: THE BEST OF FRIENDSHIPS

**Say: God wants to relate to us, but it is often hard to figure out who God is and how we see or feel God in the world around us. One of the most important ways we can understand God is to see God in our friends. If we are living as children of God, what could our friends see in us that might represent God? What are the good things about how we live, and what would cause someone to think we would be a good person to have as a friend? What kind of people do we choose as our friends?**

Hand out a pen or pencil and **Reproducible 6A** to each tween.

Ask tweens to find a space of their own away from the others and to complete this activity sheet. Give them about five minutes to finish it.

At the end of that time call them all back together.

Have an easel pad or other large sheets of paper up on a wall. Be ready to write down answers as tweens share them.

Invite tweens to think of additional answers to add to the exercise that would display being a good influence or a good friend, and see how long the list becomes. (If your group is large, divide into smaller groups to do this recording of ideas, actions, and attitudes.)

Ask a tween or other helper to read this prayer for the group:

**Pray: God of every good thing, we thank you for our friends and our families. Help us be a good influence on all those around us. Constantly remind us of who you want us to be and how you want us to live.**

## The Best of Friendships

**Supplies:**
- Reproducible 6A, page 65
- pens and pencils
- easel pad or other large sheets of paper
- marker

**Preparation:**
- Gather pens and pencils.
- Photocopy Reproducible 6A, one for each person.

## ACTIVITY 2: IN GOD'S IMAGE

Read Genesis 1:27.

Ask: What do you think of when you hear that we are formed in God's image? Do you think of our physical bodies? What we look like? How we move or think?

Invite responses.

Say: It might be easier to understand ourselves as being images of God if we think about what kind of person God wants us to be. The Bible has many stories that describe the lessons of Jesus, helping us learn by his example. God knows what is in our hearts as well as in our minds and actions. Try thinking of God's image as what's in our hearts and minds rather than our physical bodies.

Say: If people say they can see God through us, they are often talking about how we care for other people and treat other people kindly. They may see our smile, which makes them feel good, but it also reflects what's in our hearts. We are constantly shaping our lives by the thoughts and actions we choose. Now you will have some time to play with clay (or play dough). Think about shaping and forming something in God's image. End by creating a shape with your clay that represents something good about being people of God. It's good to know that God will know what we are intending to make, no matter what our forms end up looking like.

Hand out clay or play dough for each person and let him or her work.

**Leader's Tip:** If they need assistance, suggest various Christian symbols on which they can work.

## ACTIVITY 3: IT TAKES COURAGE

Read this quotation to your group: "It takes courage to grow up and become who you really are" (e. e. cummings).

Give each tween a pen and a copy of **Reproducible 6B**. After they have finished the reproducible, lead them in a discussion of the statements and answers.

### In God's Image
**Supplies:**
- Bible
- clay or play dough
- newspapers

**Preparation:**
- Cover a table with old newspapers to protect the table or give each person a piece of paper to work on.

### It Takes Courage
**Supplies:**
- Reproducible 6B, page 66
- pens or pencils

**Preparation:**
- Photocopy Reproducible 6B, one for each person.

**Leader's Tip:** If you have a large group, you may want to divide tweens into small groups with an adult leader for this discussion. Copy reproducible ahead of time to give to each leader.

## Bible Study

**Supplies:**
- Bibles in multiple versions

**Preparation:**
- none

## Walk 'n' Talk

**Supplies:**
- none

**Preparation:**
- none

**Leader's Tip:** Most tweens will not stay on the appointed topic. If you wish them to do so, you might have adult leaders float from group to group, not joining in, but just keeping tweens aware that they are to stay somewhere near the topic. If you are more concerned with the process of friends sharing while walking and talking, let it happen naturally.

## ACTIVITY 4: BIBLE STUDY

Read 1 Corinthians 16:13-14 and Proverbs 12:26. If you have several Bible translations available, read the verses aloud in each of the translations.

**Say: Has a friend ever asked you for advice? Did that person follow your advice? What does it mean to do all things in love? How would your life be different if you could really do this all the time?** (*These questions are to start tweens thinking, not necessarily for discussion.*)

Use the following questions for discussion. Have tweens open their Bibles to 1 Corinthians 16:13-14, in case they wish to refer back to it.

- What does it mean to keep alert when talking about your faith?
- What are some ways you can show you are standing firm in your faith?
- Who is the most courageous person you know? What makes that person so?

## ACTIVITY 5: WALK 'N' TALK

Sometimes it's easier to talk to people about things that matter when you aren't seated facing them and looking directly at each other. This exercise is a chance to select a conversation symbol and have a walk-and-talk discussion about it. Have tweens get into groups of three with people who have different shoe sizes from theirs (as much as possible).

Invite the trios to go outside (if you aren't already outside) and spend about five minutes as individuals finding something that represents their relationship with their parent(s). It can be a leaf, a rock, a piece of paper, and so forth.

Once they have found their representative item, they should rejoin their trio. Ask the trios to take a walk slowly and casually around the area (staying within sight of the adult supervisors), and to talk about their items as they walk. Give them fifteen minutes to walk and to return back to the starting location.

Have the full group share their experiences of the advantages and disadvantages of walking and talking at the same time. Point out that this is one technique for making important conversations more comfortable for some people.

## ACTIVITY 6: PLACES TO GO, PEOPLE TO SEE, THINGS TO DO!

Say: There are many good things you can do with your time and energy, so we are going to come up with as many ideas as possible for good places to go, good people to see, and good things to do! You will receive a copy of this list after we return home. If you ever get bored, simply look at the list and be reminded of all the great possibilities out there waiting for you!

Give each tween nine index cards. Give these instructions:

- On three of the cards, write places to go that could be interesting or fun.
- On another three, write people to see (in general, not by name, such as "a friend from church," "a neighbor you haven't seen in a while," and so forth).
- On the last three, write things to do other than wasting time, watching TV, and eating.
- See how creative, yet realistic, you can be with these ideas.

Give them ten to fifteen minutes to work on these. When everyone is done, collect the cards.

Shuffle the cards and randomly pick out one and read an answer. Repeat this process a few times so tweens can hear the wide variety of ideas that came from the group.

**Leader's Tip:** Remember to type up these lists to send home with tweens at a later date.

## ACTIVITY 7: WHO ARE THE OTHERS?

Say: OK, you know who your friends are, but who are the "others"? Are they the people who are different from you? Are they people who make choices differently from how you would? Are they people who have little or no support at home?

Give each tween a craft stick with a description statement from **Reproducible 6C.**

Say: You are receiving craft sticks with descriptions on them. You will each in turn stand up and read your stick by saying, "I am (*whatever your stick says*)." Place your stick in a pile in the center of the meeting space (*on a table, in a bowl, or on the floor*).

### Places to Go, People to See, Things to Do

Supplies:
- 3-by-5 index cards, 9 per person
- pens

Preparation:
- Gather supplies.

### Who Are the Others?

Supplies:
- craft sticks
- Reproducible 6C, page 67
- option 1: glue, scissors
- option 2: pen

Preparation:
- Gather supplies.
- option 1: Photocopy Reproducible 6C. Cut out and glue the statements to craft sticks.
- option 2: Write on craft sticks the statements from Reproducible 6C.

## Closing Celebration

**Supplies:**
- candles
- candleholders
- matches or lighter

**Preparation:**
- Gather supplies.

Say: As these are being read, think of the people you see, walk past, don't talk to, don't like, or don't understand who fit these descriptions. Do you know their names? Let's begin.

Select someone to draw the first stick. After all the sticks have been read, gather around the stick pile in the center and move into the Closing Celebration.

## CLOSING CELEBRATION
Light candles.

Say: These candles are lit for all those people who need people like us in their lives. We tend to gravitate to those who are more like us, but we want to be open to accepting all people, regardless of their background or situation or personality. They won't necessarily become close friends, but our thoughts, prayers, and smiles can warm their hearts and their days.

Pray: We are reminded today, God, of the wide diversity of people you call your children. Help us be more aware and more sensitive to those who are not like us. Help us understand the ways we can brighten their days or bring our prayers on their behalf. Show us how to model positive behavior so others around us can learn and grow as well. Keep us on track, God. Be with each of us as we return home and look toward tomorrow with new awareness, love, and respect for all people. Amen.

# The Best of Friendships

*Circle the answer that you feel best represents a sign of being a good influence on others and being a good friend.*

1. **You should help others without being asked . . .**
   a. when you feel like it.
   b. every chance you get.
   c. if it isn't too hard.

2. **When someone makes a mistake, it's best to . . .**
   a. not make fun of that person.
   b. tell that person how to do it right.
   c. laugh.

3. **When the kids around you are using offensive language, you should . . .**
   a. use the same language they use.
   b. ask them to use better language.
   c. ignore them.

4. **Laughing when someone else gets in trouble is . . .**
   a. okay if you know the person.
   b. rude.
   c. helpful in making the situation funny.

5. **Knowing the difference between right and wrong . . .**
   a. is important when making decisions.
   b. doesn't really matter.
   c. is difficult.

6. **Trying to look cool by acting bored is . . .**
   a. effective.
   b. a waste of energy.
   c. not likely to leave a good impression on others.

7. **Going to church regularly . . .**
   a. is meant for adults.
   b. is a good way to learn about God.
   c. is a way to be with friends.

8. **Helping someone understand his or her homework in a hard class . . .**
   a. is a generous thing to do.
   b. isn't worth the trouble.
   c. shows you care.

9. **Listening to music on your headphones while your leader is talking to you about something important . . .**
   a. is OK if you can still hear the leader.
   b. might offend the leader.
   c. makes the leader think you don't care.

10. **Finding positive and creative things to do with your free time . . .**
    a. is a good way to stay out of trouble.
    b. is more interesting.
    c. is too much effort.

11. **Resisting the temptation to do things you know are wrong . . .**
    a. can be hard.
    b. helps you feel good about yourself.
    c. is no big deal.

12. **Complaining about not having enough money . . .**
    a. makes you sound selfish.
    b. is OK if you need it.
    c. shows little concern for others.

13. **Doing community service for others in need, with your friends or family . . .**
    a. isn't important.
    b. is a way to show you care about others.
    c. can be fun.

14. **Not following people who are doing things that can be hurtful to others or their belongings . . .**
    a. will help you stay out of trouble.
    b. is being wise.
    c. makes you look afraid.

15. **Spreading gossip you hear about other kids . . .**
    a. is okay if it's true.
    b. can hurt their feelings.
    c. can hurt your reputation.

# It Takes Courage

*Mark your answer for each statement.*

| YES | NO | Statement |
| --- | --- | --- |
| ___ | ___ | I usually make choices that reflect what I believe to be right. |
| ___ | ___ | My friends seem to listen to what I say and care about my opinion. |
| ___ | ___ | I like to make good and responsible choices, even if others pick on me for it. |
| ___ | ___ | I like to make decisions that keep me well liked by my friends. |
| ___ | ___ | I have a lot of friends, and I don't really know a lot about many of them. |
| ___ | ___ | I have fewer friends, and I know them very well. |
| ___ | ___ | My friends sometimes encourage me to do things I shouldn't do. |
| ___ | ___ | I can often influence my friends to make good decisions and choose to do good things. |
| ___ | ___ | I am willing to work at helping my friends see the difference between right and wrong. |
| ___ | ___ | If I have to choose between the popular thing to do and the right thing to do, I tend to choose the popular thing to do in order to not lose friends. |

# CRAFT STICK DESCRIPTIONS

*Photocopy and cut apart the statements below. Glue them individually to craft sticks.*

| | |
|---|---|
| Someone you don't even notice in the school hallway each day. | Someone who eats alone in the lunch room each day. |
| Someone who wishes anyone would care about him or her. | Someone who appreciates your smile and friendly hello. |
| The owner of the dog that barks at you when you pass his or her yard. | SOMEONE WHO IS NEW TO YOUR SCHOOL. |
| The person who sits across from you in math class. | Someone who has trouble reading and learning because of medical problems. |
| Someone whose family survives on donated food from the food bank. | Someone who likes very different things from what you like. |
| SOMEONE WHO WOULD LIKE TO BE YOUR FRIEND, BUT YOU DON'T EVEN KNOW THE PERSON. | Someone who listens to music you aren't interested in. |
| An adult you see every week at the grocery store. | Someone who has no money for new clothes. |
| Someone who has no place to call home. | Someone who is lonely. |
| Someone who is clumsy in gym class. | A friend of someone you know from class. |
| Someone who needs someone to talk to. | SOMEONE WHO LIVES WITH ABUSIVE PARENTS. |

# 7 Building Christian Character

## SCHEDULE

**First Evening**

| | |
|---|---|
| 6:30 p.m. | Gather to carpool to location, if off-site (time depends on travel distance to retreat site) |
| 6:45 p.m. | Leave for retreat destination |
| Arrival on site | Get settled into sleeping areas (get beds ready & pajamas out) |
| | Gather and put on nametags, if it's a large group |
| | Give tour of facility, if needed |
| | Rules |
| | Assign buddies |
| | Introduction to retreat theme |
| 8:30 p.m. | Icebreaker |
| 9:15 p.m. | Get ready for bed (pajamas on and sitting on bed by 9:45) |
| 9:45 p.m. | Bedtime story (either from your own experience or a short one you read) |
| 10:00 p.m | Lights out and quiet |

**Full Day**

| | |
|---|---|
| 7:15 a.m. | Wake up, get dressed and ready for the day |
| 7:45 a.m. | Breakfast set-up |
| 8:00 a.m. | Breakfast |
| 8:30 a.m. | Announcements and cleanup |
| 9:15 a.m. | Morning watch (including Scripture, singing, prayer) |
| 9:30 a.m. | Review of retreat theme |
| 9:35 a.m. | Activity 1 |
| 10:00 a.m. | Juice break |
| 10:05 a.m. | Activity 2 |
| 10:30 a.m. | Activity 3 |
| 10:45 a.m. | Activity 4 |
| 11:15 a.m. | Activity 5 |
| 11:40 a.m. | Lunch preparation |
| 12:00 noon | Lunch |
| 12:45 p.m. | Lunch cleanup |
| 1:05 p.m. | Rest |
| 1:30 p.m. | Activity 6 |
| 2:10 p.m. | Snack |
| 2:30 p.m. | Activity 7 |
| 3:45 p.m. | Activity 8 |
| 3:30 p.m. | Clean up/Pack up |
| 3:50 p.m. | Closing celebration |
| 4:15 p.m. | Depart for return to church |
| ____ p.m. | Arrive at church. Parents pick up tweens to go home. |

## Supplies

- NRSV Bibles
- retreat instructions and printed materials
- nametags or materials to make them
- easel pad or other large sheets of paper
- markers
- masking tape
- paper for each person
- pen for each person
- food service items: plates, cups, napkins, spoons

*(Note: Specific items for each activity are listed by activity.)*

## Food

**Friday night snack:**
- popcorn and lemonade

**Saturday breakfast**

**Saturday lunch**

**Saturday afternoon snack:**
- veggies, dip, and drinks

# 7 Building Christian Character

**FAITHPOINT:** As Christians we are called to live righteously, treating others with the respect due to children of God, being honest and trustworthy in everything we do. Honesty or lack of honesty affects all of our relationships, even our relationship with God.

**SCRIPTURE:** Matthew 7:12; Luke 16:10; Galatians 5:22-23a, 26; Ephesians 4:25

**SCRIPTURE REFLECTION:**
Being truthful, showing respect, and being trustworthy are expressions of the character values a person holds. God calls us to be careful with each, and to speak the truth with love and respect. When we choose these values as foundations for our lives, others can see God in our actions and words. It becomes easier to deal with difficult issues if we have not complicated them with deceit, and it is easier to take on the responsibility for the choices we make. Others will want to be in relationship with us if we have good emotional and physical integrity as Jesus taught us.

**PREPARATION:**
See page 68 for the preparation check list.

**ICEBREAKER: YARN TOSS**
One person begins with a ball of yarn.

That person holds the loose end tightly and tosses the ball to a person across the circle without letting go of the loose end.

The person who catches the yarn ball has to tell one habit he or she has (not necessarily good or bad—just any habit). Then that person holds onto his or her end of the stretched yarn and tosses the ball to another person somewhere across the circle.

The catcher tells a different habit, holds onto his or her section of the yarn, and tosses the ball across the circle.

Continue crisscrossing the circle with the yarn ball until every person is holding a section of it, and a design forms in the middle.

## Yarn Toss

**Supplies:**
* yarn

**Preparation:**
* Roll yarn into a ball.

With everyone still holding the yarn, **say: We are connected by a single length of yarn, yet the pattern is intricate. Even though our lives go various directions, we can hold onto one another and be connected through God, who loves us all. God knows all about the habits we've been sharing, and God can help us sort out the good from the bad.**

The yarn pattern can be laid down and left there for now, or it can be rewound onto the yarn ball.

## ACTIVITY 1: LIES AND TRUTHS RELAY

Have space for each team to run at least fifteen to twenty feet, if possible. At the far end of the space are two batches of papers, face down. Some sheets have lies, others have truths (**Reproducibles 7A and 7B**, cut apart and pasted onto larger sheets of paper). Instead of stacking the piles neatly, place them in loose piles. Or spread them out, if there's room.

The object of this game is to match the lies with the truths.

Divide the group into two teams of ten or fewer (or four or six teams, if you have a large group). Have tweens line up in a row, one behind the other, in relay fashion.

When you say "go," the first person in each team runs to the game sheets across the room and selects one sheet from each of the two piles.

If the truth matches the lie selected, they keep both sheets and return to their relay group.

If they do not match, players must put them back in the correct pile, face down, for others to choose from. Both teams keep going until the sheets are all gone. Have each team hold up their game sheet sets, alternating team to team, and read the lie and the truth.

When this is completed, have each team (or groups of six to eight tweens with an adult facilitator) find a nearby space to sit and discuss the questions on **Reproducible 7D**.

**Say: You need to have a good memory to be a good liar because each layer of the lie gets more complicated. You have to remember what you said and who you told it to. Being truthful is much easier!**

## Lies and Truths Relay

**Supplies:**
- Reproducible 7A, page 76
- Reproducible 7B, page 77
- Reproducible 7D, page 79

**Preparation:**
- Photocopy Reproducibles 7A and 7B and cut the statements apart. Keep the lies separate from the truths.
- Glue the strips onto larger sheets of paper to make game sheets.
- Photocopy Reproducible 7D, one for each group of six to eight tweens.

## ACTIVITY 2: WHAT DOES THE BIBLE SAY?

Cut apart the Scripture cards, **Reproducible 7C**. Mix them together in a basket or other container.

The object of the game is to assemble the five Bible verses in the correct order—one verse in each of five designated areas in the room. Give one minute for each step. At the end of a minute call time.

At any time tweens may look up their Scripture in the Bible, if they draw the Scripture reference.

Ask each tween to draw a Scripture card.

Have the tweens lay down their first slip of paper by one of the numbers (any order is okay, but only pieces of the same verse can go under a number). Those who think their cards are part of the same verse should lay theirs down at the same number. Do not do any checking of verses at this point.

Again have them each draw a Scripture card, going through the same process, only this time they will not have empty areas, and they will have to attempt to match cards with the cards already by that number. If there are disputes, tell them that they can change the position of cards only by looking up the Scripture to discover the correct placement. (They can only do this if someone has drawn a Scripture reference card.)

Continue in one-minute segments until all the Scripture cards have been drawn and placed. This time they are to each stay by the last card they placed. Have each group look up their Scripture references and sort out their Scripture cards. They will probably have cards that don't belong with their Scripture. Have them put those cards in the middle of the entire area (on a table, a chair, or even the floor), and those who are missing Scripture cards can go to this pile to find the rest of their Scripture.

When all five of the Bible verses have been assembled, ask a volunteer from each group to read that group's Scripture aloud to everyone.

After each Scripture is read, ask the entire group to give examples of how that Scripture tells us to live.

### What Does the Bible Say?

**Supplies:**
- NRSV Bibles
- Reproducible 7C, page 78
- five sheets of paper, numbered 1–5
- watch with minute hand
- basket or other container
- scissors

**Preparation:**
- Photocopy Reproducible 7C. Cut apart the cards.
- Mix the cards and put them into a basket.
- Place the numbered sheets on the wall or on tables.

## Knowing Myself

**Supplies:**
- Reproducible 7E, page 79

**Preparation:**
- Photocopy Reproducible 7E for each person.

## It's Up to Me

**Supplies:**
- Reproducible 7F, page 80
- pens and pencils

**Preparation:**
- Photocopy Reproducible 7F, one for each person.

## ACTIVITY 3: KNOWING MYSELF

If possible, take everyone outside. Give each person a copy of "Think of These Things" (**Reproducible 7E**).

Give tweens ten minutes to be in silence on their own. They can walk or sit, but they must do so alone and must stay in view of supervising adults.

When finished, bring them back together to give instructions for the next activity.

## ACTIVITY 4: IT'S UP TO ME

Say: Knowing your Christian values is important, but being able to apply your values to what happens in your everyday life can be a difficult thing to do. Every time you say yes or no to someone who asks you to do something, you are making a statement about values you have chosen for yourself. You may be choosing not to do something that you know is wrong. Or you may be saying no to someone because you have already made a commitment and said yes to doing something else at that particular time, and you want to honor that commitment.

Say: Or you might just say, "Whatever," and let things happen to you without trying to have an effect on the outcome. How strong are your values? How well do you recognize what is right and what is wrong, and why? Your behavior is up to you. When it comes to your own well-being, what will you choose? Here are some things to think about. These are to guide your own thinking on these topics.

Pass out the "It's Up to Me" worksheet (**Reproducible 7F**) and pens or pencils.

Ask participants to work individually, away from others.

## ACTIVITY 5: HEALTH HABITS AND RESPONSIBILITY

Invite several tweens to do an impromptu roleplay for the rest of the group, using the scenario on Reproducible 7G. Allow them a few minutes to plan who will do what part and to look over the scenario before they start.

After they act it out, ask the audience if there are any other ways tweens could have appropriately dealt with this situation.

## ACTIVITY 6: SMALL GROUP

Have participants divide into small groups of three to five tweens for a brief discussion.

When they are ready, give them the questions to discuss on Reproducible 7H. Let them discuss each briefly.

## ACTIVITY 7: HONESTLY

Divide tweens into pairs for this exercise.

You will read each of the following questions, pausing for a short time in between for them to share their answers with their partners.

- Is there ever a time when it is good to be dishonest? (*Wait for responses after each question*.)

- Is not telling the entire truth the same as telling a lie?

- Would you rather be told a lie to spare your feelings, or the truth, even though it might hurt your feelings?

- Have you ever been lied to by someone important to you?

- Do you trust people who you know have lied to you or to others you know?

### Health Habits and Responsibility
**Supplies:**
- Reproducible 7G, page 81

**Preparation:**
- Photocopy Reproducible 7G; the number depends upon the size of your group. (You need an audience, no scenario required.)

### Small Group
**Supplies:**
- Reproducible 7H, page 81

**Preparation:**
- Photocopy Reproducible 7H, one for each group.

### Honestly
**Supplies:**
- none

**Preparation:**
- none

## Draw Christian Character

**Supplies:**
- Bible
- large sheets of paper
- colored markers

**Preparation:**
- Print the five Scripture references (right) on a large sheet of paper.

• Can you keep a strong friendship with someone who isn't truthful all the time?

• Do you think that lying about something you did wrong can be just as bad as what you did wrong?

• Are you willing to make a commitment to yourself that you will try your best to be honest at all times?

**Say: Sometimes you are the only one who will know if you have lied, except for God. Remember that if you have lied and are sorry for what you have done, you can ask God to forgive you. You can get a fresh start. If you are in the habit of telling the truth, even when it's uncomfortable, keep it up. If you have a habit of lying, you can make a change any time you want to. Honestly!**

## ACTIVITY 8: DRAW CHRISTIAN CHARACTER

Post the five Scripture references for this retreat (Matthew 7:12; Luke 16:10; Galatians 5:22-23a and 5:26; Ephesians 4:25) on a large sheet of paper where they can be seen. Make sure that each group has a Bible.

Divide your tweens into groups of three to five. Give each a large sheet of paper and colored markers.

**Ask: What's your favorite comic book character?** (*Wait for responses.*) **Why do you like this character?**

**Say: Your group is creating what you think is the best Christian character. You may use your Bibles to look up any of the posted Bible verses (or any other verse you want to use) to decide what characteristics and abilities your Christian character should have. For example, Superman is able to leap tall buildings in a single bound. Perhaps your Christian character can make three people feel good before breakfast with a dazzling smile. Use your imagination. See what unique features and abilities you can give your Christian character.**

Give the groups twenty to thirty minutes to draw their characters. Bring the groups back together. Let each group show their character and tell about its unique characteristics and talents.

## CLOSING CELEBRATION

Give tweens an opportunity to talk about some of the things that they learned or experienced during the retreat.

Say: Think about the people in your life who are good role models for you. Who are the people who help you make difficult decisions? Who are the people who make sure you are safe and taken care of? Who are the ones who teach you how to be a person of good character?

Say: We all need people who guide us when the path is unclear. We all need people to cheer us along the way and remind us we are worthy of their love and God's love.

Ask: Who are the people in your life who need someone to cheer for them? How can your positive character be a light to their path?

Pray: Patient God, we are faced with decisions every day. We make choices to follow you or to try and find our own way. Please show us the way of truth, kindness, gentleness, and self-control. May your spirit guide us along the paths that keep us true to you and true to ourselves. Amen.

### Closing Celebration

Supplies:
• none

Preparation:
• none

# Lies:

Susie told her mom she got home about 10:15 last night.

Jan told her teacher that her homework was stolen out of her backpack.

Brian told Maddy he had to go to a dinner with his family.

Brittany asked for money from her parents to buy a book she needed.

Jeff explained to Dawn that he didn't want to see the new movie.

Claire told her parents the movie was rated PG-13.

Dan said he was ready for his science test so he could play videogames.

Laura confirmed with her dad that she had money for school lunch.

Alex said that he fed the dog before leaving for church.

Taylor told his mom that his new friend went to his school.

# Truths:

Susie got home at 11:30 last night.

Jan didn't get her homework done.

Brian was at Sarah's house.

Brittany bought makeup with the money for the book she needed.

Dawn saw Jeff at the movie theater with another friend.

Claire went to an R-rated movie with older friends.

Dan flunked his science test because he hadn't studied.

Laura lost her school lunch money.

Alex's dog went hungry because Alex forgot to feed him on schedule.

Taylor's new friend was a school dropout who hung out at the mall a lot.

| | | | |
|---|---|---|---|
| In everything | is faithful also in much; | patience, kindness, | Galatians 5:26 |
| do to others | and whoever is | generosity, faithfulness, gentleness, | So then, |
| as you would have them | dishonest in a very little | and self-control. | putting away falsehood, |
| do to you; | is dishonest also in much. | Galatians 5:22-23a | let all of us |
| for this is the law and the prophets. | Luke 16:10 | Let us not | speak the truth |
| Matthew 7:12 | By contrast, | become conceited, | to our neighbors, for we are members |
| Whoever is | the fruit of the Spirit is | competing against one another, | of one another. |
| faithful in a very little | love, joy, peace, | envying one another. | Ephesians 4:25 |

# Discussion Worksheet

Which of these scenarios seemed the worst to you?

Does the size of the lie matter? Are little lies okay?

What damage can be done by people discovering you have lied?

Do you think others will trust you in the future if they know you have lied to them now?

If you were the one lied to, would you feel the same way?

# Think of These Things

- What are two of the most important things in the world to you?
- What is one thing that makes you sad?
- What is one thing that makes you happy?
- What is something you want to be able to do some day?
- What do you think you will be doing three years from now?
- What is one thing you would like to change about yourself?
- What is one of the things you like most about yourself?

# It's Up to Me

- Do you think you will try smoking cigarettes when you get a chance?

- Do you think you might be a person who develops a habit of smoking?

- Do you expect to drink alcohol when you turn twenty-one just because it is then legal?

- Do you think you will drink alcohol when you can get access to it, no matter what your age?

- Do you think you will be a person who enjoys helping other people?

- Do you expect to take time on a regular basis to worship and to be in church?

- Do you think is it important to attend church activities regularly?

- Do you feel you should be able to do dangerous things if you want to?

- Do you think it is important to be popular at school?

- Do you think that good grades are going to help you in the future?

- Do you expect to go to college and continue your education?

- Do you feel it is your responsibility to help a friend who is caught up in bad habits?

# Scenario

Some tweens are walking home from school together. They come upon a group of kids hanging out on a corner smoking. One of the group offers cigarettes to some who are passing by, and invites the tweens to stay and hang with them for a while.

Some of the walking tweens are tempted, but one or two of them remind the others that they have other things to do. They can't stop now and hang out, and urge the others to not be tempted by the smokers.

# Discussion Questions: Habits

Since you are responsible for your own behavior, what is one of your bad habits you would like to stop?

What is one habit you need to develop?

What kind of help do you need to do either of the above?

# 8 Living in Christian Community

## SCHEDULE

### First Evening

| | |
|---|---|
| 6:30 p.m. | Gather to carpool to location, if off-site |
| 7:00 p.m. | Leave for retreat destination |
| Arrival on site | Get settled into sleeping areas (get beds ready and pajamas out) |
| | Gather and put on nametags, if it's a large group |
| | Give tour of facility, if needed |
| | Rules |
| | Assign buddies |
| 8:30 p.m. | Icebreaker and introduction to retreat theme |
| 9:00 p.m. | Activity 1 |
| 9:30 p.m. | Get ready for bed (pajamas on and sitting on own bed by 9:50) |
| 9:50 p.m. | Short bedtime story in each sleeping space (either one from your own experience, or a short one you that you read) |
| 10:00 p.m. | Lights out and quiet |

### Full Day

| | |
|---|---|
| 7:15 a.m. | Wake up, get dressed and ready for the day |
| 7:45 a.m. | Breakfast set-up |
| 8:00 a.m. | Breakfast |
| 8:30 a.m. | Announcements and cleanup |
| 9:15 a.m. | Morning watch (including singing, prayer)—optional |
| 9:30 a.m. | Activity 2 |
| 9:55 a.m. | Juice break |
| 10:05 a.m. | Activity 3 |
| 10:40 a.m. | Activity 4 |
| 11:00 a.m. | Activity 5 |
| 11:40 a.m. | Lunch preparation |
| 12:00 noon | Lunch |
| 12:45 p.m. | Break |
| 1:05 p.m. | Rest |
| 1:25 p.m. | Activity 6 |
| 2:00 p.m. | Activity 7 |
| 2:30 p.m. | Snack |
| 2:45 p.m. | Activity 8 |
| 3:45 p.m. | Clean up/Pack up |
| 4:00 p.m. | Closing celebration |
| 4:30 p.m. | Depart for return to church |
| ____ p.m. | Parents pick up tweens |

## Supplies

- NRSV Bibles
- retreat instructions and printed materials
- nametags or materials to make them
- easel pad or other large sheets of paper
- markers
- masking tape
- paper for each person
- pen for each person
- food service items: plates, cups, napkins, spoons

*(Note: Specific items for each activity are listed by activity.)*

## Food

- Friday night snack
- Saturday breakfast
- Saturday lunch
- Saturday afternoon snack

# 8   Living in Christian Community

**FAITHPOINT:** Jesus calls us to live in Christian community, devoting our lives to righteous living.

**SCRIPTURE:** Ecclesiastes 3:1-8; Acts 2:42; and Ephesians 5:15-16a

**SCRIPTURE REFLECTION:** (also for Closing Celebration) Our entire lives are made up of a series of choices. What we do each part of each day totals up to be our lifetime. God wants our lives to be filled with experiences and relationships that bring joy and truth both for us and for the communities in which we live. Jesus reminds us in the Book of John that he is the gate by which we are saved and brought close to God. John 10:10b says, "I came that they may have life, and have it abundantly." However, it is up to us to use what God has given us to create lives of joy and to bring a better life to others. You can begin to understand the challenge of making wise decisions that make your lives and the lives of those around you more fulfilling.

Getting involved in activities with other people that help you build your faith in God and express what's inside you can help others understand you and appreciate you more. Community activities require cooperation and working together. Experiencing a wide range of activities helps you develop as a well rounded and responsible person. It is an opportunity to build up one another.

Being involved in religious activities gives tweens an opportunity to seek good counsel from adults other than their parents and to see Christian behavior modeled as a chosen lifestyle.

## PREPARATION:
See page 82 for the preparation check list.

## ICEBREAKER: NICKNAMES
Ask each tween to tell the group a nickname he or she has been called and the story behind it—perhaps who started it and why. If anyone does not have a nickname, he or she should make one up.

When everyone has had a turn, ask the group to identify anyone they think used a fake nickname. Confirm with that person whether or not his or her nickname is true.

### Nicknames
**Supplies:**
• none

**Preparation:**
• none

## A Time for Everything

**Supplies:**
- Bibles
- Reproducible 8A, page 91
- two paper sacks or baskets
- scissors

**Preparation:**
- Photocopy and cut Reproducible 8A into strips. Keep the first half of each phrase in one group and the second half in another.
- Divide the slips into two paper sacks.
- If you have a large number of participants, you will need to repeat the process to make more sets.

## Game Show

**Supplies:**
- easel pad or other large sheets of paper
- marker

**Preparation:**
- none

## ACTIVITY 1: A TIME FOR EVERYTHING

Place Scripture strips **(Reproducible 8A)** into two sacks—one sack for the first halves of the phrases, the second sack for the finishing halves of the phrases.

Divide tweens into two teams. Give each team a Bible. Have them turn to Ecclesiastes 3:1-8.

Instructions: One person from each team will run forward and draw a phrase out of the sack. The two go to a table and place their phrases in the correct places. How fast can the group build the entire Scripture in the correct order? Time them.

**Ask: What are some things you expect to see changing in your life in the next few years?**

## ACTIVITY 2: GAME SHOW

Divide six tweens into two teams of three and ask the questions below for both groups to answer. Each team gets one minute to answer. The team members must confer and come up with a group answer.

The rest of the tweens are the viewing audience, and they watch the game as they cheer on the participants.

Ask one tween volunteer to keep track of the team results in two columns on a large sheet of paper.

- Name two things you do each day that begin with the letter *R.* (*read, run, rest, rap, relate, relax, and so forth*)

- Name three good choices you made yesterday.

- Give the first names of three people you think make good use of their time.

- Name two things you do that are creative.

- Name two more things you do that are creative.

- How many members of your team had a meal with their parent(s) yesterday?

- How many of your team had a discussion with their parent(s) yesterday?

## ACTIVITY 3: DRAWING OUR LIFELINES

Give each tween a pencil and a piece of paper. Have tweens turn their papers sideways. Invite each tween to draw a long line in the center of the paper, going from left to right, with a vertical line about two inches tall at each end (example below).

Ask tweens to write their birth date at the left end of the line, and today's date at the right end of the line. Explain that this line represents their lives from birth to now.

As a group, brainstorm ideas of major events (both good and bad) that happen in people's lives. This will give them ideas to use on their own individual timelines.

**Say: Think about these things: Has there been an especially good time in your life that stands out? Has there been an especially difficult time in your life that stands out?**

Have tweens label special times or events in their own lives in the approximate times of their lives, if they know when the events happened. If they don't know, or you want to make it easier, they could put things from the early years on the left half and things more current on the right half, in any order they can remember them.

When everyone is done, invite tweens into a time of showing and telling about their lifelines. Be ready to assist those who find this difficult by asking them questions about specific points on their lifeline.

When each person has shared his or her lifeline, use tape to hang the lifelines on the walls for all to see.

### Drawing Our Lifelines

**Supplies:**
- easel pad or other large sheets of paper and marker for brainstorming
- one piece of long paper (14 or 17 inches long) for each person
- pencils
- fine-point markers in various colors
- tape

**Preparation:**
- Gather supplies.

## Choose Your Action Relay

**Supplies:**
- Reproducible 8B, page 92
- paper sack or basket, one for each team
- scissors

**Preparation:**
- Photocopy and cut apart Reproducible 8B.
- Make more actions slips, if needed.
- Gather sacks or baskets.

# ACTIVITY 4: CHOOSE YOUR ACTION RELAY

Make as many sacks or baskets of "Action Slips" **(Reproducible 8B)** as you need to have multiple teams. There are ten actions described, but you may add more or make up your own as well.

Divide your group into relay teams of ten or fewer people.

Ask teams to line up behind each other for a relay.

At the far side of the room, place a paper sack or basket with a set of instruction slips in it for each relay team.

Give these instructions to the teams:

- The first person on each team will run to the team sack across the room.

- You will pull out one slip of paper and read the directions.

- Drop the instruction slip on the floor beside the sack and do whatever the instruction says.

- When done, run back to your team and touch the next person in line.

- That person runs to the sack and draws a slip of instructions, and so forth.

- Your goal is to be the team that follows the directions accurately and completes the actions quickly for all the slips in the sack.

- OK, first runners . . . go!

## ACTIVITY 5: WHOSE CHOICE?

The objective is to identify what decisions tweens make and what choices are influenced or determined by parents or others. Some choices, like how they treat others, are their own responsibility. Other choices are privileges earned with age and experience, and some may be prompted by God.

Write each of the circle choice items on a separate circle of paper and tape each circle to the wall, easel pads, or a door. If you have other ideas to add during the activity, tape them up as well.

Give each tween a set of stickers. (Dot stickers are the least expensive.) Explain that the dot stickers are "yes" answers. Invite the tweens to put "yes" dots on the circles that have descriptions that they get to make their own choices about.

Invite a brief discussion in response to their answers.

If your group has a wide age range, divide into groups of similar ages for the discussion time.

**Leader's Tip:** Some tweens will complain about how few choices they get to make on their own. This can be an especially difficult age, because tweens tend to feel that they are ready for more privileges than their parents think they are ready for. Tweens need to understand that they do have choices about how they treat other people.

**Ask: Do many of you seem to have similar limits or similar freedoms and privileges? Who do your choices affect? Are your choices based on your Christian values? What choices or privileges do you look forward to handling on your own in the next couple of years?**

### Whose Choice?

**Supplies:**
- 8½-inch circles of paper
- masking tape
- marker
- small dot stickers, enough for each person in the group to have fifteen

**Preparation:**
- Write each choice item (from list below) on a separate circle of paper and tape each circle to the wall. Add ideas of your own.

**Circle Choice Items:**
- What clothes you wear to school
- How late you stay out at night
- Going to church
- How you spend your money
- Cleaning your bedroom
- Trying out for school or community sports
- Going to a church group
- How you treat other people
- Having a friend visit in your home
- Auditioning for the school play
- Attending family events or activities
- Doing something risky where you might get injured
- Choosing who you hang out with
- Playing the music you like

## Balancing Life

**Supplies:**
- one dry two-by-four piece of lumber eight to ten feet long
- markers with sharp tips

**Preparation:**
- Gather supplies.
- Have the board on a table, with markers spread out in front of the board.

## Getting on Board

**Supplies:**
- two-by-four board used in the previous activity
- carpeted floor or grassy outdoor area

**Preparation:**
- Place the board on the floor with plenty of room all around it for people to gather.
- Have adult spotters arranged in advance to stand on both sides of the board, back a short distance, to be catchers in case people fall.

## ACTIVITY 6: BALANCING LIFE

Say: Having a well-rounded life most likely means that you are active in a variety of activities. Think about all the activities you do that fill up your typical week.

Say: Think about home, family, neighbors, school, sports, music, art, pets, tasks, fun, work, and time wasters.

Say: Your life is sometimes a balancing act, such as making the best choices, adjusting schedules, and moving from activity to activity.

Say: Now, one at a time come forward to the balance beam (two-by-four board), think of one answer to this question, and write your brief answer on the board. Let's see how many different answers we can come up with to fill the board.

Ask: What are the things you do that fill up your typical week? Tell us one thing and write it on the board.

Continue until everyone has had a chance to write on the board.

## ACTIVITY 7: GETTING ON BOARD

Say: While it is important to be well-rounded in your experiences and knowledge, it is also important to be aware of how much you can handle well and how much is too much. As you get older, it becomes more and more your own responsibility to make decisions about which activities to do and which to pass up. Some of the decisions will be privileges earned by good and responsible behavior. Some of the decisions you make may not work out as planned. It's all part of learning, and we do the best we can.

Say: Let's see how much our balance beam can handle. Every person who wrote something on the balance beam needs to stand on the plank without touching the floor (or ground, if you are outside). Come forward one at a time and take your place on the board. When the board becomes crowded, you will need to help one another to stay balanced and to get everyone on the board.

Invite one person to begin.

## ACTIVITY 8: RITES OF PASSAGE

Say: When you're riding in a car on a longer trip, you might ask, "Are we there yet?" At this age in your lives you are experiencing times when you get additional privileges and responsibilities or begin to focus on particular interests or needs in your community or the world. Some of the times you experience are major turning points or launch pads for what's next.

Give the tweens the leaves from **Reproducible 8C** that you have written statements on, photocopied, and cut out.

Say: We are going to watch this tree blossom with leaves that represent possible rites of passage in your lives that you may already be experiencing or are quickly approaching. Different ones tend to happen at different ages or circumstances, but many are common to most people.

Ask: Can someone tell us what a *rite of passage* is? (*A rite of passage is a ritual that marks a change in a person's life, often, but not always, marked by ceremonies surrounding the events.*) You will be receiving several leaves with various rites of passage on them. They represent changes in our lives.

Say: As you receive your leaves, one at a time, you may go to the tree, read your leaves out loud, and place them on the tree branches to help fill out our tree. Someone will be there to hand you pieces of tape (*or have loops of tape all over the tree ready for the leaves*).

Let the tweens complete the tree.

Say: It is clear by looking at this tree that there are lots of transitions in going from childhood to youth and beyond. Many of them will involve school, home, church, and friends. You are fortunate to have a group of people right here who care about you and who will encourage you as you transition and celebrate many rites of passage through the next several years. You can make good choices about how you use your time in response to the many opportunities you will be offered.

Say: The most important thing to remember to do as you make transitions is to take God with you. God won't leave you behind, and you need to be sure you don't leave God behind. You are partners—family—in this journey we call life.

### Rites of Passage

**Supplies:**
- Reproducible 8C, page 93
- roll of brown kraft paper or mural paper you can paint
- markers
- scissors
- masking tape

**Preparation:**
- Make a large flat paper tree out of kraft or mural paper—trunk and branches, no leaves.
- Make a lot of leaves using the leaf pattern on Reproducible 8C (several for each person).
- Tape the tree to a sheet of mural paper that is attached to the wall.
- Write one rite of passage on each leaf. It's okay to use them multiple times, since there are multiple people. (See the list on Reproducible 8C.)
- Assign someone to handle the masking tape process for the leaves.

---

### Closing Celebration

**Supplies:**
• NRSV Bible

**Preparation:**
• Mark Bible passages.

**Leader's Tip:** You may wish to assign different people (adults or tweens who are good readers) to read the various Bible passages.

---

## CLOSING CELEBRATION

As a wrap-up of this retreat, read Ecclesiastes 3:1-8; Acts 2:42; and Ephesians 5:15a-16. Share the following Scripture reflection with the group:

Our entire lives are made up of a series of choices. What we do each part of each day totals up to be our lifetime. God wants our lives to be filled with experiences and relationships that bring joy, justice, peace, and truth, both for us and for the communities we live in. Jesus reminds us in the Book of John that he is the gate by which we are brought close to God. John 10:10b says, "I came that they may have life, and have it abundantly." However, it is up to us to use what God has given us to create lives of joy and to bring a better life to others. You can begin to understand the challenge of making wise decisions that make your lives and the lives of those around you more fulfilling.

Getting involved in activities with other people that help you build your faith in God and express what's inside you can help others understand you and appreciate you more. Community activities require cooperation and working together. Experiencing a wide range of activities helps you develop as a well-rounded and responsible person. It is an opportunity to build up one another.

Being involved in church activities gives you an opportunity to seek good counsel from adults other than your parents and to see Christian behavior modeled as a chosen lifestyle. Take advantage of this time with people who care about you and how you grow into adulthood. Don't miss the adventures and passages to freedom you will gain with time and with God.

**Pray: God, there are so many changes and transitions as we live and grow in community with others. We are comforted in knowing you are right here beside us through all of these days and years ahead. There is so much to learn and to experience, and we don't want to miss any of it. Thank you for your continuous love and guidance in our lives. Amen.**

# A Time for Everything

*Ecclesiastes 3:1-8*

*For everything there is a season, and a time for every matter under heaven:*

| | |
|---|---|
| a time to be born, | and a time to die; |
| a time to plant, | and a time to pluck up what is planted; |
| a time to kill, | and a time to heal; |
| a time to break down, | and a time to build up; |
| a time to weep, | and a time to laugh; |
| a time to mourn, | and a time to dance; |
| a time to throw away stones, | and a time to gather stones together; |
| a time to embrace, | and a time to refrain from embracing; |
| a time to seek, | and a time to lose; |
| a time to keep, | and a time to throw away; |
| a time to tear, | and a time to sew; |
| a time to keep silence, | and a time to speak; |
| a time to love, | and a time to hate; |
| a time for war, | and a time for peace. |

# Action Slips

*Photocopy and cut apart into separate slips for the sacks.*

Do seven jumping jacks, clapping your hands together at the top of each one.

Hop on one foot back to your relay team without tipping over or putting your other foot down.

Sing loudly one full verse of "Old McDonald Had a Farm."

At the same time pat your head with one hand and rub your stomach in circles with the other hand.

Hold your arms straight out and twirl around five times.

Do the hula.

Run back to your team and grab the second person in line and play leap frog to the sack and back.

Count out loud by threes, up to forty-five.

Yell the name of a nursery rhyme.

Run back to your relay team to get three other people and play "Ring Around the Rosie" together.

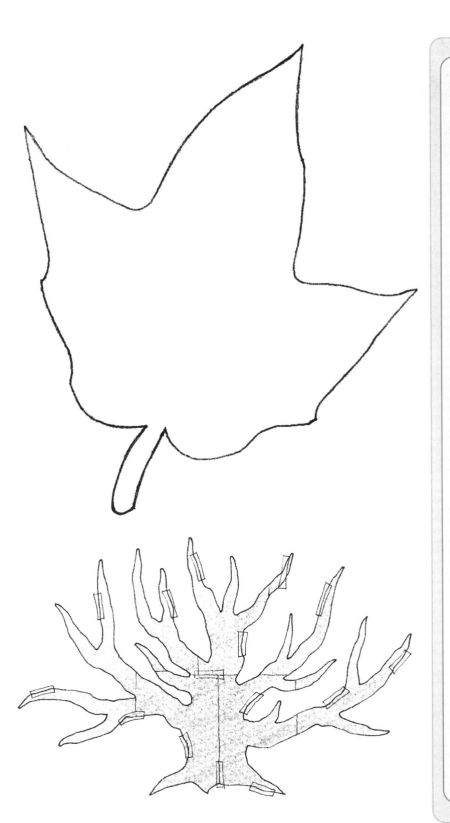

**Rite of Passage List
to Print on Leaves:**
(*Add others as you wish.*)

Going from elementary to
middle school

Baptism

Church membership

Confirmation

Choosing clothes you buy

Youth group retreats

Community service

Social action

Writing to your government
officials

Choosing foods you will or
won't eat for a reason

Assisting in worship

Helping serve Communion at
church

Going some places on your
own

Earning some of your own
money

New level of adventures
(such as whitewater rafting)

Deciding how to use your
free time

# Retreats and Developmental Assets Relationship Chart

Each retreat in this book helps tweens' developmental process. By looking at the Developmental Assets chart, you will see which of the retreats in this book deals with which types of Developmental Assets.

| RETREAT | DEVELOPMENTAL ASSETS |
|---|---|
| Retreat #1: Resisting Temptation | Asset #35: Resistance Skills |
| Retreat #2: Family Support and Communication | Asset #1: Family Support<br>Asset #2: Positive Family Communication |
| Retreat #3: Peaceful Solutions | Asset #36: Peaceful Conflict Resolution |
| Retreat #4: A Passionate Heart | Asset #39: Sense of Purpose |
| Retreat #5: Doing Justice: A Service Retreat | Asset #21: Achievement Motivation (in Christian service)<br>Asset #26: Caring<br>Asset #27: Equality and Social Justice |
| Retreat #6: Being a Positive Influence | Asset #15: Positive Peer Influence |
| Retreat #7: Building Christian Character | Asset #29: Honesty<br>Asset #30: Responsibility |
| Retreat #8: Living in Christian Community | Asset #17: Creative Activities<br>Asset #18: Youth Programs<br>Asset #19: Religious Community |

# 40 Developmental Assets

Search Institute has identified the following building blocks of healthy development that help young people grow up healthy, caring, and responsible.

| Category | Asset Name and Definition |
|---|---|

## External Assets

### Support

1. **Family Support**-Family life provides high levels of love and support.
2. **Positive Family Communication**-Young person and her or his parent(s) communicate positively, and young person is willing to seek advice and counsel from parents.
3. **Other Adult Relationships**-Young person receives support from three or more nonparent adults.
4. **Caring Neighborhood**-Young person experiences caring neighbors.
5. **Caring School Climate**-School provides a caring, encouraging environment.
6. **Parent Involvement in Schooling**-Parent(s) are actively involved in helping young person succeed in school.

### Empowerment

7. **Community Values Youth**-Young person perceives that adults in the community value youth.
8. **Youth as Resources**-Young people are given useful roles in the community.
9. **Service to Others**-Young person serves in the community one hour or more per week.
10. **Safety**-Young person feels safe at home, school, and in the neighborhood.

### Boundaries & Expectations

11. **Family Boundaries**-Family has clear rules and consequences and monitors the young person's whereabouts.
12. **School Boundaries**-School provides clear rules and consequences.
13. **Neighborhood Boundaries**-Neighbors take responsibility for monitoring young people's behavior.
14. **Adult Role Models**-Parent(s) and other adults model positive, responsible behavior.
15. **Positive Peer Influence**-Young person's best friends model responsible behavior.
16. **High Expectations**-Both parent(s) and teachers encourage the young person to do well.

### Constructive Use of Time

17. **Creative Activities**-Young person spends three or more hours per week in lessons or practice in music, theater, or other arts.
18. **Youth Programs**-Young person spends three or more hours per week in sports, clubs, or organizations at school and/or in the community.
19. **Religious Community**-Young person spends one or more hours per week in activities in a religious institution.
20. **Time at Home**-Young person is out with friends "with nothing special to do" two or fewer nights per week.

## Internal Assets

### Commitment to Learning

21. **Achievement Motivation**-Young person is motivated to do well in school.
22. **School Engagement**-Young person is actively engaged in learning.
23. **Homework**-Young person reports doing at least one hour of homework every school day.
24. **Bonding to School**-Young person cares about her or his school.
25. **Reading for Pleasure**-Young person reads for pleasure three or more hours per week.

### Positive Values

26. **Caring**-Young person places high value on helping other people.
27. **Equality and Social Justice**-Young person places high value on promoting equality and reducing hunger and poverty.
28. **Integrity**-Young person acts on convictions and stands up for her or his beliefs.
29. **Honesty**-Young person "tells the truth even when it is not easy."
30. **Responsibility**-Young person accepts and takes personal responsibility.
31. **Restraint**-Young person believes it is important not to be sexually active or to use alcohol or other drugs.

### Social Competencies

32. **Planning and Decision Making**-Young person knows how to plan ahead and make choices.
33. **Interpersonal Competence**-Young person has empathy, sensitivity, and friendship skills.
34. **Cultural Competence**-Young person has knowledge of and comfort with people of different cultural/racial/ethnic backgrounds.
35. **Resistance Skills**-Young person can resist negative peer pressure and dangerous situations.
36. **Peaceful Conflict Resolution**-Young person seeks to resolve conflict nonviolently.

### Positive Identity

37. **Personal Power**-Young person feels he or she has control over "things that happen to me."
38. **Self-Esteem**-Young person reports having a high self-esteem.
39. **Sense of Purpose**-Young person reports that "my life has a purpose."
40. **Positive View of Personal Future**-Young person is optimistic about her or his personal future

## Retreat Permission Slip
*Please return this completed form to the church office.*

Tween's Name: _____

Grade: _____ Age: _____

Address: _____

_____

E-mail: _____

Phone: _____ School: _____

School address: _____

School phone: _____

Allergies: _____

Other medical conditions: _____

_____

Parent(s) or guardian(s) name(s): _____

Home phone: _____ Work Phone: _____

Cell phone: _____ Pager: _____

Please provide names of persons to contact if parent(s) or guardian(s) cannot be reached.

1. Name: _____ Home Phone: _____
   Work Phone: _____ Cell Phone: _____
2. Name: _____ Home Phone: _____
   Work Phone: _____ Cell Phone: _____
3. Name: _____ Home Phone: _____
   Work Phone: _____ Cell Phone: _____

The above has my permission to participate in the _____
(church name here)

Church tween ministry events between September 1, 20___ and August 31, 20___. I also

understand that _____ is not liable should injury come to my
(church name here)

child. I give permission for emergency medical care to be given by a hospital should my child

need such treatment before I am contacted.

Signature of parent or guardian:

_____

Insurance company and number: _____

Doctor's name: _____

Doctor's address: _____

Doctor's phone: _____